BIG GAME SHOOTING IN THE INDIAN EMPIRE

BIG GAME SHOOTING IN THE INDIAN EMPIRE

C. H. STOCKLEY

GYAN

Published by

GYAN

Gyan Publishing House
5, Ansari Road
Daryaganj, New Delhi-110002
Phone: 011-47034999, 9811692060
E-mail: books@gyanbooks.com

Distribution Network
gyanbooks.com
India, USA, Canada, UK, Australia

ISBN: 978-93-7225-183-8 (PB)

First Published, 1928

2nd Impression 2025

Printed at: Gyan Press, Delhi.

BIG GAME SHOOTING IN THE INDIAN EMPIRE
Author: C. H. STOCKLEY

BIG GAME SHOOTING IN THE INDIAN EMPIRE

BIG GAME SHOOTING IN THE INDIAN EMPIRE

BY

LIEUT.-COLONEL C. H. STOCKLEY

D.S.O., O.B.E., M.C., F.R.G.S., F.Z.S.

LONDON

CONSTABLE AND COMPANY LTD.

1928

PREFACE

Since the publication of Kinloch's fine book some forty years ago, no general book on Indian Big Game Shooting has been produced, though there are several dealing with particular areas.

The object of the present volume is to try and fill this want at a price within the reach of the ordinary soldier-sportsman of India, and to give an idea of the appearance and habits of the various species, with advice as to the best way of setting out to shoot them. Questions of cost have therefore necessarily limited the size of the book, and elaborate life histories and descriptions, with full bibliological references, have had to be omitted.

The book is intended primarily for the man of limited means who follows his game on foot, and wants to obtain the essence of sport by doing his following up and finding himself.

I hope this object will be fulfilled.

CONTENTS

PART I

PART II

PART I

GENERAL AND INTRODUCTORY

INDIA has been renowned for its big game since the days of the first European adventurers who set foot on its shores, and though nowadays it is the fashion to speak of it as shot out, this is not really so. Although the game has diminished greatly in a few districts in the last fifty years, yet there are still large tracts of country from which only an occasional sportsman takes toll; while the abandonment of a number of small cantonments in favour of the concentration of troops in big stations, has saved the game in many good districts from serious depletion. For there are many men in India who will go out after big game if it be within reach of a day's ride, but will not give up the pleasures of cantonments for several days at a time. Then the ethics of the sport have changed in favour of the game. Females and immature males are shot only by the ignorant and by malefactors inspired with a thirst for killing and utter indifference to true sport; so that one no longer hears of bags such as that of a certain ducal slaughterer, whose chit for "seven dozen ibex" his former shikari (a doddering old patriarch) showed me in Kashmir some twenty years ago. Such a hecatomb would no longer be tolerated by public feeling, even where the law permitted, and such places are now few and far between.

Preservation of game in India has made great strides, but has unfortunately been directed almost entirely against the sportsman, whose methods by no means tend to the extermination of game, though they do incline to cause a deterioration in heads, unless judicious rules are enforced limiting the head of game to be shot in certain areas, and closing altogether for a period of years, those showing signs of over-shooting.

Shooting rules of this type are particularly well drawn up

in countries like the Central Provinces, Central India and the United Provinces, under the "block" system; and in Kashmir under the "nullah" system: though in the latter country, to my mind, the preservation has been unnecessarily overdone in the matter of limiting the number of head shot, and not sufficiently in the way of closing ground too easily accessible, in order to force sportsmen to spread out further afield.

But throughout India, without exception, the chief enemy of the game, the native shikari to wit, is not sufficiently controlled.

Whereas the British sportsman brings money into a district, and, in nine cases out of ten, helps to foster a better feeling between European and Indian tending to counteract the evil influences of sedition, the native shikari sits up over a water hole or beside a jungle path, slaying hind or fawn without thought of anything but the meat and hide, which he will sell to the nearest buyer. Sometimes in the hills they will drive an animal into deep snow and club it to death. One native shikari will do more damage to the game in one hot weather than a dozen British sportsmen in the whole of their residence in India. No one would wish to prevent the native from protecting his crops (which is easily done with any old firearm with half the barrel sawn off), and this is the usual excuse given for according him facilities for destruction; yet elephant, which will destroy acres of sugar-cane or rice in a single night, are protected to such a ridiculous degree, that in certain parts of Southern India and Burma they are a never-ceasing menace to property, and sometimes to life as well, and these animals the native does not shoot.

The native shoots for pecuniary profit; for he sells hide and meat, and, in certain pernicious cases, the head as well.

In the last twenty years a regular market has sprung up for the sale of trophies. Heads from Kashmir, the United Provinces and the Central Provinces, find their way through Rawalpindi and Sialkot, Cawnpore, Allahabad and Harda, to the big shops at Bombay; and in a few cases to Calcutta. They are sold, at the most amazingly high rates, to globe-trotters, who sometimes save a lot of money by purchasing their "trophies" at a middleman's up-country shop. These middlemen have a regular clientele of native shikaris from whom they buy heads. What pleasure the eventual purchaser derives from these " trophies " is unintelligible to the sportsman, whose recreation and chief pleasure in life he is helping to destroy ; but the fact remains that the sale continues.

Now the remedy is simple, and has often been pointed out. Make the sale of any portion of a wild animal, hide, horns or meat, a criminal offence, and the trade will cease. This will not affect the cultivator's right to protect his crops, and carnivora would of course be excepted. It is no use laying down a five-rupee penalty for an infringement of the law, as is proposed in the Indian Game Preservation Act which has been drafted and not passed. The native shikari can get Rs.20 for a bison hide, the same for his head, and Rs.30 for the meat. These prices I can personally vouch for as having been paid in the Belgaum bazaar when I was stationed there. The usual rate of remuneration for the meat of a sambhar in Ootacamund is about Rs.30, and the hide will fetch Rs.12 to Rs.15. Government has protected birds by the Act forbidding the sale of their plumage, and the enormous profits to be made are well demonstrated by the fact that, in spite of the heavy fines inflicted, smuggling still continues. Now trophies are too bulky to be easily smuggled, and the trade would be too risky to continue, if equally strong measures were taken as has been done for the birds.

Surely it is not too much for the sportsman to ask that, as he pays a licence and much other money for his sport, this amount of return should be made him. At present the money acquired through the sale of licences seems to be taken for the higher education of inefficient babus ; for all that is done is that the Forest Department is saddled with a lot of extra work, or a few native game rangers are appointed at ridiculously inadequate salaries who will come and make a nuisance of themselves to the white man in order that their officiousness may reach the ears of their superiors and show how hard they are working. Their pay they augment by a personal system of licences (of which the profits are also personal) to their native brethren ; and, in some cases, they not only assure the destroyers against legal proceedings, but actually assist them in their nefarious work. Sportsmen would gladly pay higher licences if it would ensure more efficient protection.

Not one native in a thousand will trouble to go shooting if he cannot obtain profit by it, either pecuniary or in kind, and if the opportunity for profit is removed, the cause of destruction is removed also. Stop the demand, and the supply will cease.

From the above remarks I must except Burma, for there the native destroys little game, except a few thamin which he hunts with dogs.

I have said that there is still a lot of game left in India, but let me warn men who may think of coming out from England to shoot, that they will have little success unless they have friends in India to help them.

Nearly all game is in reserved forests, and there are not more than enough of these to go round. They may get invited to some native potentate's shoot, where they will see a very fine " tamasha ", which will afford much fun. Otherwise let them go to Kashmir, where they will be able to obtain an efficient shikari to run their trip for them, though on an 80 per cent advance of the cost at which a resident of India will do it. We who have to spend the greater part of our lives in India, consider the big game shooting as one of the chief compensations for exile, and are, very naturally, not over anxious to be crowded out of the best grounds by wealthy strangers from other countries. If a good sportsman comes out from home during the cold weather with introductions to people stationed in a good mixed game district, he will be shown grand sport with duck and snipe, antelope and gazelle ; and all in a glorious climate. He would thus get to know men who would help him to some big game shooting later on in the spring or summer.

If a man be invited by another experienced in Indian big game shooting to accompany him on a trip, let him not miss the chance. Africa may show more beasts, but not half the sport. *Crede experto.*

Unfortunately the ethics of big game shooting have deteriorated in one way of late years, and that is in the matter of using mechanical appliances to make things easier for the hunter. This does not make for real sport.

The Sport of big game hunting lies in the means adopted to

bring the hunter up to the game, not in the shot or in the trophy secured. It lies in pitting one's own natural faculties, brains and endurance against those of the game, and securing an *easy* shot by means of them and not by the use of searchlight or motor-car. Shooting big game from a motor is not sport, though it may be found amusing by some, but is merely the outcome of laziness. There should be few thrills and moments of great excitement, with the power of modern rifles to back the hunter, and such thrills usually mean that there has been mismanagement in the approach and consequent unnecessary suffering to the beast.

Sport again cannot be measured by the size of the trophy obtained. A 40-inch ibex from Kishtwar is as fine a trophy as a 45 from Baltistan, and provides just as good sport. The oldest and finest male is picked out to shoot, because he is usually the wariest of his kind ; while finding and selecting an individual is more of a test for the hunter's abilities than shooting an undersized herd beast, and consequently the sport is greater.

If a shot cannot be obtained without mechanical help, then leave the beast alone. If the animal is not fully adult or does not carry a sufficiently good trophy, then leave it alone. It is infinitely better to come back with no trophies at all than a number of undersized specimens. Of course, accidents will happen even to the most experienced, but that does not affect the general principle.

In dealing with other sportsmen be generous-minded, and do not try and cut them out of good shooting by means which you would not care to have employed against yourself. It is the custom in India that the first comer on the ground has the sole right to shoot the nullah, jheel or other defined area. The man himself must be there : it is no use sending on a camp to occupy the ground and following on later, though this is an unfair trick which is sometimes practised and is forbidden by the game laws in Kashmir. Of course, if a reserved block has been taken and the fee paid, it immediately becomes the sole property of the man who has rented it for the period of the licence, and no one else can camp in it.

Civil officials, such as Deputy Commissioners and Divisional

Forest Officers, from whom licences are obtained and blocks booked, are usually very helpful, and I think the jealous man (not sportsman) who tries to keep all shooting for himself by unfair use of his official powers, has almost vanished. There were notorious and unpleasant examples of this, one or two in high places, who are still remembered to their discredit. One of the few I ever came across, having succeeded in freezing out every one else from the reserved forests in his district, and hearing that I was coming to shoot some unreserved ground near by, rode over it all the day on which I arrived, letting off a Mauser pistol or carbine, in order to frighten the game off it and so spoil my shooting.

But that sort of thing is now, I think, a thing of the past, and I have met with the greatest courtesy and assistance from most Forest Officers, who are very hard-worked, yet frequently spare the time to write valuable advice which they are under no necessity to impart.

Space has not permitted any attempt to give very detailed accounts of any districts or game animals, and the following books are recommended with reference to the particular districts shown against them :

BURMA. *Big Game Shooting in Upper Burma*, by Major G. P. Evans.

NILGIRIS. *Sport in the Nilgiris and Wynaad*, by Fletcher.

CENTRAL INDIA. *Wild Animals in Central India*, by Dunbar Brander.

Shikar Notes for Novices, by the Hon. A. W. Best.

ASSAM. *Wild Sports in Assam*, by Col. Pollok.

KULU, LAHOUL and SPITI. *The Sportsman's Manual for Kulu, etc.*, by Col. Tyacke.

KASHMIR. *The Tourist's and Sportsman's Guide to Kashmir and Laduk*, by Col. A. E. Ward.

The Tourist's Guide to Kashmir, by A. E. Neve.

Other useful books are : *Records of Big Game*, by Rowland Ward,
The Indian Field Shikar Book, by Burke, and
The Game Animals of India, by Lydekker.

These last two books contain a good many errors, but they are very useful, and I have to acknowledge my indebtedness to them and all the other books mentioned above.

I would strongly advise every man who goes big game shooting to take up some branch of natural history as a hobby. It adds immensely to the interest of a trip, and assists the hunter to observe the habits of big game rightly ; without such intelligent observation no one can obtain real sport. Being led up to a beast by other men is not much to be proud of. With regard to observation, it should be noted that the habits of animals often vary considerably with the district in which they are found, and because they do not do a thing in one district, that is no real reason that they should not do it in another. Dunbar Brander, in his *Wild Animals in Central India*, has set an excellent example in his way of recording such things as he has seen, and comparing them with the observations of others. There should be no " trailing of coat tails " when discussing such an interesting subject.

I would also advise that as many species as possible be shot. Each has its own peculiar habits and development of faculties to be defeated, and adds to the knowledge and resource of the hunter ; while each also takes him to varying types of country and climate, of which there is such a wonderful profusion in India.

THE SELECTION OF A SHOOTING-GROUND

The considerations which govern the selection of a shooting-ground are many and various, but the principal are these. Firstly, whether any particular species of game is desired; secondly, the period of time available for the trip; and thirdly, the season of the year.

In any case, unless a particular species of game is wanted which cannot be otherwise reached, the number of days' marching to be done should not exceed the actual number of shooting days, and one day's marching to two days' shooting is the limit for good sport and comfort.

The most favourable seasons for shooting each particular animal is recorded with its description later on, but the following general principles should be observed.

Where the method of pursuit is by tracking, the season to select is that of the early rains, when the ground is soft enough to take an impression, the jungle open before the undergrowth has grown too thick, and the dead leaves soft enough to prevent their being too noisy underfoot.

For beating, the hot weather before the rains is the time; for there is then little water and, the undergrowth having died and the leaves fallen, the jungle is open. Thus the game sticks to thick patches with water and shade near together, and is easy to mark down.

For Himalayan shooting, go when the snows are melting and the fresh green grass begins to grow. As the season advances the snow disappears up to the perpetual line, thus throwing open such a large extent of mountain-side for the animals to roam over, that they are hard to find.

For still hunting, in which the stags of the plains and foot-hills are the usual objects of pursuit, January to March are the

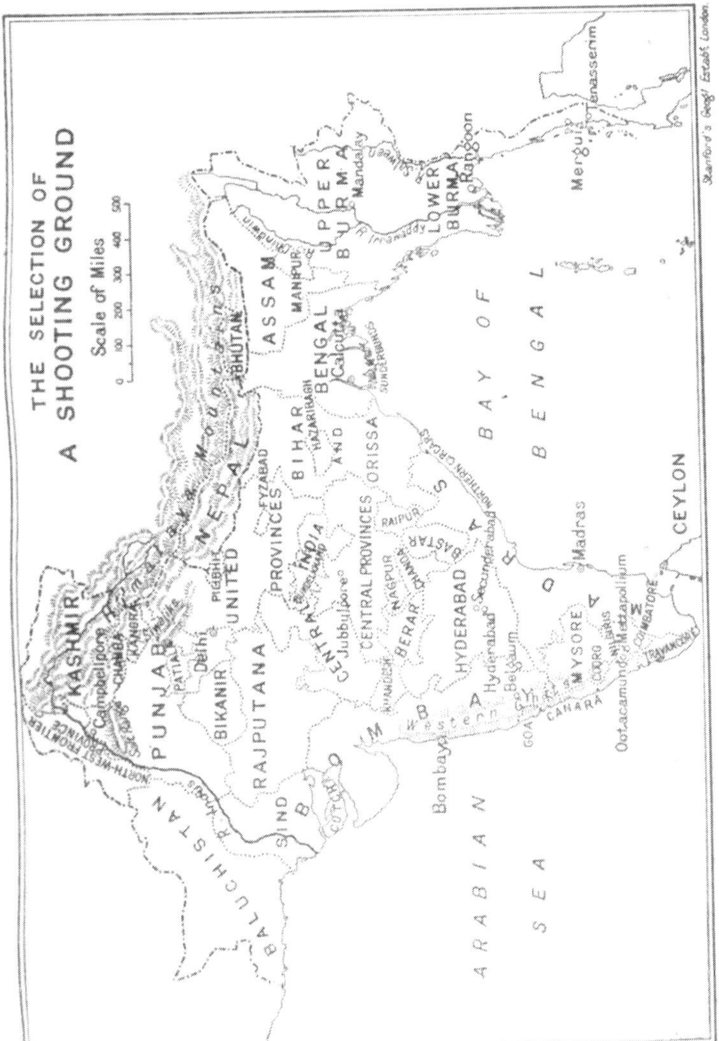
THE SELECTION OF
A SHOOTING GROUND
Scale of Miles
0 100 200 300 400 500
KASHMIR
PUNJAB
RAJPUTANA
BIKANIR
UNITED PROVINCES
NEPAL
BHUTAN
ASSAM
MANIPUR
BIHAR AND ORISSA
BENGAL
Calcutta
UPPER BURMA
LOWER BURMA
Mandalay
Rangoon
Mergui
Tenasserim
CENTRAL INDIA
CENTRAL PROVINCES
RAIPUR
BASTAR
NAGPUR
BERAR
HYDERABAD
Hyderabad
Secunderabad
Jubbulpore
Delhi
Campbellpore
SIND
BALUCHISTAN
CUTCH
BOMBAY
Bombay
MYSORE
MADRAS
Madras
Ootacamund
Mettapollium
COIMBATORE
TRAVANCORE
CANARA
GOA
Belgaum
NORTHERN CIRCARS
CEYLON
BAY OF BENGAL
ARABIAN SEA
NORTH-WEST FRONTIER PROVINCE
Stanford's Geog! Estab! London.

best months ; as the climate is favourable, the grazing area for the animals is limited, and the stags are mostly in hard horn ; though this latter point varies greatly with species and district.

Kashmir and the rest of the Himalayas are treated in a separate chapter, so we will now confine ourselves to considering the various districts of the plains.

The greater number of the Indian jungles are divided into " blocks ", to shoot in which a permit has to be obtained from the Deputy Commissioners or Forest Officer of the district. A fee varying from five to fifty rupees is charged for this permit, which may cover one block only or every block in the district, and which allows the holder to shoot for a period of 10 to 30 days (according to local rules) in the particular block allotted to him.

Each permit allows the holder to shoot a limited number of each species of game, and there is a further limit imposed as to the number that may be shot in each block. Thus, if a permit be granted allowing the holder to shoot two bison, and block limit be also two bison one of which has already been shot last year, then the permit-holder must shoot his second head in some other block for which he must apply for another permit, but for which he may or may not have to pay a fee according to the district.

A block may be applied for not more than three months in advance, and it is advisable to apply as early as possible, for good blocks are usually taken up well in advance.

In most districts there is a rule in force to the effect that a native forest guard must be taken on to his ground by each sportsman. This guard is there to see that the Game and Forest Regulations are complied with : he may be of great assistance or an unspeakable nuisance ; it is a toss-up.

Permission to shoot in a native state is almost always obtained through the British Resident or Political Agent. A licence fee has usually to be paid.

In Burma, Rs.150 has to be paid for a permit to shoot in " Reserved Forest ", and Rs.300 to shoot in a " Special Game Reserve ". Half these fees are returned when the licence form is sent back, properly filled in, to the Forest Officer concerned, provided that the game laws have been complied with.

In every case the local Deputy Commissioner or Forest Officer should be written to for information as to the latest alterations in the game laws, and the blocks closed to shooting.

Some districts in India are subject to particular local disadvantages at certain periods of the year. Thus the valley of the Bhawani river (at the base of the Nilgiris) is a malarial death-trap for most of the year, while leeches render life a misery at certain seasons in some districts. Inquiries should be made about such matters; for, after all, one goes shooting for pleasure, and it is idiotic to take unnecessary risks of having the pleasure of a trip ruined by illness. All these local plagues abate considerably or entirely disappear during some season of the year.

Now as to expense.

The most expensive form of shooting is undoubtedly beating. Tiger-shooting in Hyderabad or the Central Provinces, for instance, is a most expensive form of sport. Then marching is most expensive when coolis have to be used, less so when pack animals are taken, while bullock carts are the cheapest of all forms of transport.

The cost of one's licence and the railway journey must be considered, including the by no means inconsiderable item of extra luggage.

I do not think that the cost of a shooting trip of two or three months' duration anywhere in India will be less than Rs.500 a month except to the very experienced. Expenses will be less if two or more shoot together, but sport will probably be less also. Big game shooting is a selfish sport, and, except for beating, a one man shoot is the best.

A longer trip will cost less per month on the average, unless a large amount of marching is done; for supplies are usually cheap, and the cost of the railway fares and licence are spread out over several months. The cost of food varies greatly with the district, and if supplies are scarce more food will have to be carried, and so the cost of transport increases, and tinned stuff also adds to the expense.

Thus in estimating the probable cost of a trip the items should be put under the following heads:

1. Licence.
2. Railway journey, including servants' fares and extra baggage.
3. Journey from railhead to shooting-ground.
4. Marches while on ground.
5. Wages of personal servants.
6. Wages of shikaris, trackers and beaters.
7. Bakshish.
8. Outfit.
9. Stores.
10. Supplies.

Numbers 1, 2 and 3 are easily ascertainable.

4. This is a most variable item. In the hills it is usually the most expensive item of the trip, while in the plains it is often one of the smallest, as camp is not shifted so often and carts can be frequently used.
5. Treat your servants liberally and take at least two, or one and an orderly. My own personal servant gets free food and an extra five rupees a month, also a pair of boots and some clothing on starting.
6. This varies from eight annas to a rupee a day for shikaris and trackers, while beatérs vary from three to six annas a day.
7. Bakshish is a constant difficulty. Over-liberality is as much to be avoided as parsimony. My own principle for shikaris is to fix a reward for every head of a certain measurement, plus so much an inch for every inch over that measurement. Thus, I offer Rs.5 bakshish for a 40-inch ibex, and Rs.2 for every inch over that length, so a 44-inch head brings in Rs.13 to the shikari. With tiger and panther the fairest way is to give the Government reward to the shikari and distribute an equal amount among the beaters or other helpers. Bakshish to lumbardars and such like petty officials is much more difficult to fix, but as a rule, if satisfied, I give the equivalent of a day's pay of my personal servant plus a small bonus for every cart, pony or cooli supplied to me. Bakshish to coolis is based on the length of the march and its general difficulty,

nothing being given for a short easy march. In Chamba, for instance, liberal rates are laid down by the state for each march, most of the marches being ridiculously short.

8. Outfit is more expensive for the hills than the plains, as camp coolis in the hills have to be taken on permanently and have to be given chaplis and some clothes on starting.
9. Stores are dependent on the supplies available in the district in which the trip is to be made. Be liberal to yourself.
10. Supplies. This is the cheapest item of the trip. Fifty rupees a month will cover their cost in almost any part of India.

Now let us look at a couple of estimates of current expenditure for a month.

(*a*) NORTH CANARA

Shikari, 28 shooting days at 12 as. a day .	Rs.21	0	0
2nd Shikari, 28 shooting days at 8 as. a day .	14	0	0
2 coolis, 28 shooting days at 4 as. each a day .	14	0	0
Supplies	40	0	0
Stores	120	0	0
Personal Servant	30	0	0
2nd Personal Servant	25	0	0
Bakshish	30	0	0
Carts for marching	10	0	0
Petty cash and etceteras	25	0	0
	Rs.329	0	0

(*b*) HYDERABAD OR CENTRAL PROVINCES

Shikari, 25 shooting days at 12 as. . .	Rs.18	12	0
2nd Shikari, 25 shooting days at 8 as. . .	12	8	0
40 Beaters, at 3 as. each for 10 days . .	75	0	0
Supplies	40	0	0
Stores	120	0	0
Personal Servant	30	0	0
2nd Personal Servant	25	0	0
Bakshish	100	0	0
Marching (carts)	20	0	0
Petty cash and etceteras	25	0	0
	Rs.466	4	0

The estimate for beaters is moderate; that for bakshish also as there are more claimants, and a tiger will cost at least Rs.50 in bakshish if got by beating. The marching is probably under-estimated in both. Petty cash covers machan-making. I have put down nothing in either estimate for beasts for tying up.

Both these estimates are on the moderate side, and to these must be added the cost of licences, the journey by rail and road to the shooting-ground, and the cost of outfit, cartridges and probably photographic accessories.

The Canara district is probably the cheapest of any in which to shoot, Hyderabad the most expensive. An estimate for hill-shooting is given in the next chapter.

Now let us get down to examining the game lists of individual districts: from these I have omitted both leopard and barking deer, as being practically ubiquitous.

1. Burma.—Holds much game and a very large area of good shooting.

(*a*) Elephant. Widely distributed, and may be shot on special permit.

(*b*) Rhinoceros. The small two-horned species is widely distributed but scarce everywhere.

(*c*) Buffalo. Occurs sparingly in three districts in Lower Burma.

(*d*) Bison. Plentiful in most districts wherever there are hills.

(*e*) Tsine. To be found in most parts of Burma. Plentiful in dry zone and Chindwin valley.

(*f*) Sambhar. The Malayan species is to be found nearly everywhere.

(*g*) Hog Deer. In the valleys of the larger rivers, particularly where there is much kaing grass.

(*h*) Thamin. Plentiful in the dry zone; local north and south of it.

(*i*) Bear. The Himalayan black bear is distributed throughout the hills west of the Salween valley up to Arakan. It is nowhere plentiful, and is replaced further east and in Tenasserim by the Malayan species.

(*j*) Serow and goural. Very local.

Kiun Lake, Ladakh 15,000 ft. Ovis ammon ground behind.

Kiang on the plain near the Indus ford at Nimu Mud, Ladakh.

To face page 16.

(*k*) Tapir. In Tenasserim and Mergui.

(*l*) Tiger and leopard are everywhere.

From the above it will be seen that the game of Burma is large and varied, but—there are many disadvantages. The language difficulty is more acute than anywhere in India, where an interpreter is almost always to be found who can speak English or some other language known to the sportsman. Then shikaris of any ability are few and far between, so that the sportsman may have to do nearly all his own tracking. Tiger and leopard are very hard to obtain, as they have plenty of game to prey on, so seldom kill cattle, and the jungle is so heavy and continuous that beating is impossible. Then in many parts the monsoon is so heavy as to render shooting impossible during its full force. The jungle is too thick to make it worth while shooting till January, and wages are high and supplies scarce. So much for the objections. On the other side we have the quantity of game, and the immense area available for shooting. Then the climate is delightful in the hills from January to April or early May, and throughout the dry zone (between latitudes 18° and 22°, excluding Arakan) from May to August, the same period being excellent for the Chindwin valley. To my mind there is no finer country for the man who has already had some experience, but I would not recommend it to the novice.

2. Travancore (native state).—Elephant (protected), bison, sambhar and chital (poor heads of both), tiger, sloth bear, Nilgiri tahr. The best months are February to May. Climate feverish on the whole. Supplies good. Well worth a visit, as the bison heads are very fine. Communications are indifferent.

3. Coimbatore (block system).—Elephant (special permit), bison, sambhar and chital (poor heads of both), Nilgiri tahr, blackbuck (not worth shooting), tiger and sloth bear. Supplies good. Worth a trip from February to May or early June. Bison and tahr are good.

4. Mysore (native state).—Elephant (protected), bison, sambhar and chital (fair heads), tiger and sloth bear. Good on the whole. February to June 15. Very fair mahseer fishing.

5. Nilgiris (no blocks).—Elephant (special permit), bison on foot hills and in Wynaad, sambhar and chital (poor heads), Nilgiri tahr, tiger (not plentiful) and sloth bear. From the point of view of the bag alone, the Nilgiris are not worth a trip nowadays, but in the cold weather the climate is glorious, and a tahr and two or three sambhar (with poor heads unfortunately) may be obtained in lovely surroundings. There is good mahseer fishing in the Bhawani at the foot of the hills near Mettapollium, and excellent rainbow trout (May to September) in the streams west of Ootacamund. There is a close season for big game from May to September inclusive. Bison are fairly numerous in the Bhawani valley, but fever is very bad, the jungle full of prickly pear, and elephants a perfect curse, the cows continually interfering with the sportsman. Supplies good. Licence, costing Rs.50, from the Nilgiri Game Association.

6. Canara (block system).—Elephant in S. Canara (protected), bison, sambhar and chital (fair heads), tiger and a few sloth bear. Bison are well worth trying for in the early rains, May and June, but the jungle is so thick and continuous as to make the bagging of tiger and leopard very difficult. Pretty sport may be had with sambhar and chital in the bamboo jungle, particularly near the Kalanadi river, which holds plenty of mahseer. Supplies scanty, and Canarese the only language.

7. Western Ghats.—Bison, sambhar (fair heads), tiger, sloth bear. The bison are good, and the shooting often open stalking on the hill-sides, but there is not much shooting-ground, and the Belgaum garrison work most of it. A Goa permit, which may be obtained through the British consul, will open a lot more good ground on the Portuguese side of the ghats. Season, February to August. Supplies, scarce.

8. Hyderabad (native state).—Bison (fair), sambhar, chital, tiger, sloth bear. The tiger shooting is the thing, but it is mainly reserved for the officers of the Secunderabad garrison and the state officials. It is not worth while for the ordinary man to try, unless through the good offices of some official. Best season, December to May, but shootable throughout the year.

9. Berar.—Bison, sambhar, chital, tiger, sloth bear. This

IN THE NILGIRIS.

To face page 18.

used to be a very fine shooting country, but the great improvement in the roads and communications generally and a couple of bad famines led to a great diminution of the game. The chital heads were particularly fine. Season, January to June.

10. KHANDESH.—Bison, sambhar, chital, blackbuck, chinkara, four-horned antelope, tiger, sloth bear. The Bombay jungles have suffered much from poaching, over-shooting and famine; but there are still many fine heads left, and preservation has saved much good ground. Season, January to June. The only Indian lions live in the Gir forest in Cutch.

11. CENTRAL PROVINCES (block system).—Bison, sambhar, chital, swamp deer, blackbuck, chinkara, nilgai, four-horned antelope, tiger, sloth bear. The Central Provinces still hold a lot of game in spite of the reckless shooting which went on before proper preservation was begun: but as it is only since then that railways have begun to traverse the wilder portions, there is much good shooting still to be had. In those localities where game is still plentiful, a good block is very hard to get, and a large number of the best blocks are always booked up by district officials and officers of the Jubbulpore or other garrisons. The heads of sambhar, chital and swamp deer are very good. The country is often park-like and fairly open, and supplies plentiful in most districts. A shoot can be carried out at any season of the year, but December to March are the best months for the stags, March to May for tiger, and June and July for bison.

12. THE NORTHERN CIRCARS OF MADRAS.—Bison, buffalo, sambhar, chital, tiger, sloth bear. A good but wild and feverish country. Communications are poor and supplies scarce. Information about the shooting is hard to obtain and the district little visited by sportsmen. March to July the best season.

13. CENTRAL INDIA, RAIPUR, NAGPUR, CHANDA (block system).—Buffalo, bison, sambhar, swamp deer (scarce), chital, blackbuck, chinkara, nilgai, four-horned antelope, tiger, sloth bear. Buffalo are nowhere plentiful. Shooting can be carried on throughout the year, but the heaviest part of the monsoon turns all the streams into raging torrents, making moving about very difficult. The country also becomes very feverish.

May, June and the first half of July are the best months, though the stags should be tackled earlier.

14. Bastar (native state).—Buffalo, bison, sambhar, chital, tiger, sloth bear. Very hard to get at, as no railway touches it at present, and the roads are bad. A permit must be obtained through the resident. Season, March to July 15.

15. Assam.—Elephant, rhinoceros, buffalo, bison, sambhar, swamp deer, hog deer, tiger, bear (Himalayan, black) and thamin in Manipur. This is a very fine sporting country, but suffers from a very heavy rainfall, want of communications and very thick jungle, a lot of which is high grass. These disadvantages, coupled with a paucity of supplies, make the country very difficult for the non-resident. Elephants are absolutely essential for shooting in some places, owing to the high grass. But, nevertheless there are districts where buffalo or bison (not together) can be shot on foot and really fine sport obtained. The best time for buffalo is December to February, and for bison it varies with the locality, but in any case the greatest force of the rains should be avoided. The mahseer fishing is very fine, especially in late autumn.

16. Bengal.—Tigers are very plentiful in the Sunderbunds, where there are also a good many buffalo, large numbers of chital, with poor horns, and a few rhinoceros. Tigers are hardly to be shot in any other way than by sitting up; and even then a natural kill is necessary, for they live in luxury on the deer and pig. Buffalo do not seem to carry very good heads, and are usually pretty truculent. A launch, or boat of some kind (hired from Calcutta), is indispensable, and a trip should be made in the cold weather.

Northern Bengal holds good bison and tiger shooting, swamp deer in places and sambhar in most jungles (including the Malayan species), while bear are plentiful. The jungle is very thick, and game, consequently, hard to get up to. February to May is the best season.

17. Hazaribagh is notorious for man-eating tigers, leopards and wolves, but holds little horned game.

18. Orissa holds buffalo, bison, tiger, sambhar, bear and

STRAIGHT-HORNED MARKHOR GROUND. NORTH-WEST FRONTIER PROVINCE.

MARKHOR GROUND. ASTOR.

To face page 20

blackbuck. A good sporting country of moderate extent, where game is very local. Season, November to June.

19. United Provinces and Bundelkhand.—Tiger, sloth bear, sambhar, chital, swamp deer, hog deer, blackbuck, chinkara, nilgai. In the hills: serow, goural, tahr, bharal, black bear, a few red bear. The United Provinces constitute as pleasant a sporting country as any man could wish for, and there is shooting to be had all the year round, either in the hills or plains. The tiger shooting of the Doon and Terai is famous, the Philibhit and Fyzabad districts provide wonderful mixed bags, and the Siwaliks add goural and serow to the game list. A morning walk in the Siwaliks may produce anything from a tiger to a mouse deer.

The Himalayan shooting is dealt with in the next chapter.

The best season for the United Provinces is the latter half of the cold weather, at which time of year the small game shooting is as good as anywhere in the world. The fishing, both in river and tank, is also excellent all over this country.

20. Rajputana.—An agglomeration of native states in which permission to shoot is usually very hard to obtain. There is good tiger shooting in the east, and very fine sambhar are to be shot in the south-east portion of the area; but the immense herds of blackbuck are the great feature of the north and west, where there are also many chinkara. Sloth bear also are plentiful. Myriads of sandgrouse congregate in the cold weather, which is the time for all shooting, as the hot weather is fierce and the scanty rains cause little alleviation of the heat.

21. Sind.—Notable mainly for its small game shooting, it also holds the Sind ibex and the oorial (locally known as "gud") amongst the bare stony hills. There are hog deer on the islands in the Indus, and chinkara in the deserts. The hot weather is impossible for shooting. The Persian gazelle also occurs.

22. Baluchistan.—A few straight-horned markhor and oorial comprise the big game list of Baluchistan. The cold weather is the only shooting season.

23. Punjab.—In this are included Kangra, Kulu, Lahoul and Spiti; these are all discussed in the next chapter. Other

than in the Himalayan regions the Punjab holds little game. There are oorial in the Salt Range and the hills west of Campbell-pore, and fine blackbuck and chinkara to be shot in Patiala and towards the Bikanir border. A heavy licence has to be paid in Patiala. There is excellent small game shooting in many districts, and much fine mahseer fishing.

24. The North-west Frontier Province.—Straight-horned markhor, oorial and chinkara, scattered here and there, is all the big game in this province. The animals have a hard time of it, as guas are many. There is good small game shooting in places, and some excellent fishing.

This ends the survey of the main shooting areas of India, and now the intending hunter has only to make choice of a district for a trip and then pay for his licence. More information will be found about the individual beasts in the latter half of the book.

HIMALAYAN SHOOTING

SHOOTING in the higher mountains gives, perhaps, greater pleasure to its devotees than any other branch of the sport in India. The actual bagging of a good head does not entail such a high degree of efficiency in the science of finding and following the quarry as does tracking dangerous game, but the sport is carried on in such magnificent surroundings and delightful climate that it attracts more votaries than the more dangerous and exacting branch of big game shooting.

Kashmir is the " ultima thule " of mountain sport and the finest big game field of the world, so we will take it first.

In spite of reckless slaughter in past days, Kashmir still holds a great deal of game, though one has to go a long way for good heads of most species. The valley itself holds only barasingh, leopard, black bear, a few red bear, and serow, the few ibex still existing in the watershed of the Jhelum being rigorously protected. The valley, therefore, from the big game shooter's point of view, is hardly worth a visit except for the barasingh shooting, which opens on September 15 and closes on March 14. In addition to the barasingh shooting, good sport may be had in winter with leopard and serow, while the small game shooting is magnificent. The following licences are in force:

(a) SUMMER LICENCE	Rs.125
Barasingh	2
Markhor	2
Ibex	3
Tahr	4
Goural	4
Ovis ammon	2
Tibetan antelope	4
Tibetan gazelle	1
Bharal	4
Shapu	2
Serow	1
Red bear	2
	31

(b) WINTER LICENCE	Rs.75
Barasingh	1
Markhor	2
Ibex	2
Tahr	3
Goural	3
Ovis ammon	1
Tibetan antelope	3
Tibetan gazelle	1
Bharal	2
Shapu	2
Serow	1
Red bear	1
	22

Both the above licences cover small game shooting, and there is no limit to the number of leopard, snow leopard, black bear, wolf and pig which may be shot on them.

A special licence of Rs.50 (which may not be repeated) allows the holder to kill an additional head of any animal but markhor or *Ovis ammon*.

One musk-deer may be shot on a special licence costing Rs.30. This may be repeated.

A licence costing Rs.40 covers black bear, leopard and pig.

The following districts are under special regulations as far as the number of guns is concerned :

1. KAJ-I-NAG and SHAMSHIBRI.—Six guns allowed in each period.

2. ASTOR.—Ten guns in each period.

3. LADAKH.—Twelve guns in the first period, twenty in the second, including three in Changchemmo in each period.

In each case the first period is from April 15 to July 14, and the second the following three months.

Guns for the first period are allotted by priority of arrival of applicants in Kashmir ; for the second period, by priority of application on or after January 1 of each year.

Nullahs (in Ladakh, blocks) are always allotted to applicants in order of arrival, in Kashmir, the earliest comers having the choice.

There are also one or two nullahs closed in every district, but this principle does not seem to be carried far enough, as, instead of reducing the number of head of a species to be shot, because nullahs near Srinagar are being depleted, such nullahs should be closed and sportsmen forced to go farther afield. Thus the number of bharal allowed was reduced from six to four a few years ago, because sportsmen habitually went to the same nullahs, and consequently heads became scarce. Bharal are very plentiful in the Upper Shyok valley, in parts of Rupshu, and even in some nullahs quite a short distance from the main Srinagar-Leh road : I have counted two hundred from my tent door in one place. In Zanskar bharal swarm in places. Then the number of ibex was reduced from four to

In Kishtwar: Ibex ground.

Bharal ground in Zanskar.

To face page 24.

three for exactly the same reason in 1913. Sportsmen and their shikaris are sheep-like in the way in which they go year after year to the same nullahs : often a nullah actually opening on the main track will be found to hold good heads, no one having had the originality to think of trying it for years past. In 1911 I went two marches off the main road into a bit of country ten marches from Srinagar, as against the twenty to the Upper Shigar, where everybody flocks. Only one sportsman had visited that district in the past three years, and in spite of the fact that I was at least a month too late, I shot a 41-inch ibex in the first nullah I tried, a 42-inch ibex in the next, and then, putting up a limit of 45 inches, I failed to find a head up to my standard in the other three I tried, though I saw several more 40-inch heads.

To prevent the shooting of immature heads the following standard lengths of horn have been fixed, below which sizes the shooting of each species is forbidden:

Markhor, 44 inches; ibex, 35 inches; *Ovis ammon*, 38 inches; shapu, 24 inches; bharal, 23 inches; barasingh, 35 inches and 10 points.

The last two are distinctly open to criticism. There are innumerable fully adult and really old bharal rams in Zanskar and the Shyok valley, which do not reach the 23-inch standard by an inch and a half; and bharal are so numerous in these districts that this shortness of horn cannot possibly be ascribed to over-shooting.

With barasingh, the fixing of any limit of size is liable to prevent the shooting of old stags past their prime, whose heads have gone back. Now the shooting off of such animals is necessary to maintain the standard of heads. The limit as to points prevents the shooting of switch-horns, but these are fortunately so rare at present, that it is hardly necessary to consider them; but, on the other hand, I myself shot an 8-pointer with 40-inch horns, while another of 44 inches was shot in the Sind valley some years previously, and was exhibited at the Vienna exhibition. There can be no doubt as to these two beasts being fit to shoot, yet in 1911 I should have committed an offence against the game laws by shooting a stag which was considered a fine specimen in 1905.

But enough of preservation and game laws. Let us now consider the sporting potentialities of each district.

(*a*) The first shooting district seen is almost always that of the Kaj-i-Nag. This beautiful range of mountains lies on the right bank of the Jhelum, and as the sportsman travels to Srinagar from Chakoti onwards, the mouths of the markhor nullahs are opposite him, only a few hundred yards away. Good heads are now hard to get, even though a six-gun limit is enforced; but occasionally very fine bucks are shot, and as the ground is so close it is a cheap shoot. I fancy, from what I saw in 1912 and 1926, that winter poaching by the villagers is largely responsible for the scarcity of shootable bucks. Goural, leopard and black bear are fairly plentiful; and there are some red bear, which may not be shot in that district. The ground is mostly wooded, and in spring and summer the open parts of the hill-sides are beautiful with masses of wild flowers.

(*b*) The next district under special rules is Astor. This is the most expensive district in which to shoot, as all supplies have to be carried, extra permanent coolis engaged, and the rate for local coolis is Rs.2 per march. It is an excellent sporting district, as it holds fine markhor and ibex and red bear, while there is an excellent chance of bagging a snow leopard. There are a good many shapu also, but their heads are poor as a rule.

Next door to Astor is Chilas, whose game list is the same, and for which three permits are issued every year. The chances of a good bag are not nearly as good as in Astor.

(*c*) Ladakh is the third and last district under special rules. The game list is as follows: *Ovis ammon*, shapu, bharal, ibex, Tibetan antelope, Tibetan gazelle, snow leopard, lynx and wolf. *Ovis ammon* is, of course, the king of all hill game, and nearly every sportsman who goes to Ladakh does so with a view to securing a specimen of this grand sheep. All the ammon ground is now divided into blocks except Changchemmo, which has a limit of three guns (included in the total allowed in Ladakh). None of these blocks are nearer than twenty marches from Srinagar, and some are another six or seven marches further on. Two *Ovis ammon* may be shot on each licence, and bharal are the only other species met with on the ground, except Tibetan gazelle in a few blocks and, in Changchemmo, Tibetan antelope. Of course snow leopard, lynx or wolf may perhaps be met with and bagged, but they cannot be counted on. Very pleasant sport may be had in the Indus valley below Leh with ibex, bharal and shapu, good heads of all being obtainable, though the bharal are hard to find. The first period of the year is the best for the Indus valley shooting and the nearer blocks containing ammon, while Changchemmo and the further parts of Rupshu are best visited in late summer. There are a few yak to be found in Changchemmo, but they may not be shot in Kashmir territory.

Before entering Ladakh every sportsman has to sign a declaration on his word of honour that he will not attempt to cross into Tibetan territory.

The Upper Shyok and Nubra valleys are not included in the " block " system, and hold some very fine ibex and bharal. I would strongly recommend this country to a man who has plenty of time at his disposal.

(*d*) The first of the " open " districts is Haramosh. It holds very fine ibex and markhor, but has the disadvantage of being nearly a month's march distant from Srinagar. The marches from Skardu onward are very bad going, and the shooting-ground difficult above the ordinary. It is consequently impossible of access for men on short leave. It should be visited early in the year, and the best shooting is to be had in the winter, though April and May are also excellent months. Later in the year, when the opening of the Deosai route shortens the journey by seven marches, the game has retired into the recesses of the higher mountains, and is much harder to find and approach.

(*e*) Baltistan is a big country and still holds plenty of good ibex, though heads of 44 inches or over are now scarce ; nevertheless, a careful shot ought to make sure of his ibex averaging 40 inches or a little over. Good shapu are few and far between, and red bear only occasionally seen, but are on the increase. I would recommend any one who wants to make certain of getting good specimens of ibex to go to Baltistan. Although the more famous nullahs have been shot so regularly for many years that they no longer hold big heads, yet there are others, sometimes opening on to the main road itself, which no one has the enterprise to try. These are often entered by some sportsman who finds all the nullahs of best repute occupied in advance of him. As often as not his despised last resource provides him with finer heads than are obtained by those occupying the more famous localities. The ground, as a rule, is pretty easy going in Baltistan, and the climate lovely.

(*f*) Zanskar is a barren country with few supplies, which holds bharal in plenty, and some large herds of ibex in a few favoured localities. The bharal heads are poor, but the ibex are often quite good, and an average of 40 inches should be attained. Zanskar is rather hard of access, but is well worth a trial via Suru and the Pense pass, or Kishtwar and the Umasi La.

(*g*) Kargil and Suru. There are some fine ibex still to be had in this district, though communications are indifferent. There is very good red bear ground up the Shingo Shigar, and a few in Suru in the hills between the Umba La and the Bhot Kol passes. There are a few bharal near Lamayuru, and shapu extend from there as far west as Kharbu. A country well suited for short leave if very big heads are not expected.

(*h*) Kishtwar is to me the most delightful shooting-ground. The marching is hard and supplies are scanty, but the scenery is grand and game plentiful. The climbing is usually very stiff. The game list includes ibex, tahr, goural, serow, musk-deer, black bear, red bear and leopard. I have shot the first six in the same nullah, and both the other two were present also. There are barasingh in the nullahs round the Sinthan and Marbal passes, and a few barking deer in a hill-side jungle about ten miles east of Kishtwar. The barasingh shooting is only good very late in the season. The Chenab runs right through Kishtwar, and every nullah on the north side holds ibex, which improve in horn the farther east you go. They are nowhere very plentiful, and about 44 inches is the limit of size, while 40 inches should be obtained in Padar (the eastern

IBEX GROUND. BALTISTAN.

SIND IBEX GROUND.

To face page 28.

division of Kishtwar) by any painstaking sportsman. There are some ibex on the left bank of the Chenab near Atholi, but good heads are unusual. Tahr are plentiful nearly everywhere, and I have seen three hundred or more from the road up to Padar in one day. Much of the tahr ground is very stiff, but the sport is grand. Goural are everywhere, and serow in most nullahs. There are black bear in every nullah, and fine red bear are common. Musk-deer are in many localities, but are terribly poached, while barking deer are absolutely protected.

One thing to be noted about Kishtwar is that the season is short. The mountains run up from the Chenab to 20,000 feet in a few miles, and the Chenab only averages about 4000 feet above sea level. The best ground faces south and the snow melts off quickly, so that there is soon a very large expanse of mountain open to the game. The mountains are so precipitous and broken that even the natives of the country are at a loss in a great deal of it, while as soon as the grass grows long it droops flat on the hill-side, presenting a surface almost impossible to traverse.

Kishtwar is a small country, scantily populated ; coolis are hard to get, and supplies few and far between. A twelve-gun limit with no restriction on nullahs would be an immense benefit to it. Get in early in the year and no finer sport can be imagined.

(*i*) Tilel. Ibex and red bear. Much over-shot in the past and little good now.

(*j*) Wardwan. This district threatened to become quite shot out at one time, as it was so easily accessible, and suffered heavily from the reckless massacres perpetrated by some shooters in early days ; but it became unfashionable and little visited, and a lot of big nullahs were closed, so that now it is well worth a visit for ibex alone, while there are also a good few red bear. There are good barasingh in the nullahs on the west side low down the river. Tahr and goural are to be had about fifteen miles above the junction of the Wardwan with the Sinthan river.

This ends the Kashmir shooting-grounds, so let us pass to the other Himalayan districts to the south-east.

1. The first is Chamba, a small native state on the east of Kishtwar. This used to hold a great deal of game, but was rather over-shot for a while: now it is, if anything, over-preserved. There are over thirty nullahs to shoot in which permission must be obtained from the Rajah himself, and these closed nullahs include all the best ground in the state. In fact it is little good going to shoot in Chamba unless such permission is obtained. The game list includes ibex (40 inches very rare), tahr, goural, serow, red bear and black bear. The numbers of each allowed on licence vary from year to year, but are always very limited. Musk-deer are entirely protected. The licence costs Rs.30.

The great advantage of Chamba is its accessibility, by rail to Pathankot and thence by road via Dalhousie. A tonga will reach Dalhousie in six hours, and it is then only 21 miles by a good bridle road to Chamba town. It is a beautiful country, and well worth a visit if the bag is not too serious an item in the holiday. The shooting is also cheaper than Kashmir.

2. Next on the east we come to Bara Bagahal, a tiny little bit of British territory at the source of the River Ravi, which holds a few quite decent ibex and red bear. It is a favourite shoot of the Gurkha officers stationed at Bakloh, and is well worth a visit in spring before the shepherds crowd into it.

3. Then comes Kulu. This is a famous fruit-growing valley with a delightful climate, but the big game has been sadly depleted, largely by residents who have killed the once numerous red bear without mercy. Ibex never were plentiful, but there are a few tahr and goural still to be got. Black bear and leopard are both fairly common.

Kulu is now very strictly preserved, only four permits being issued to non-residents.

4. Lahoul, which, like Kulu and Bara Bagahal, forms part of the Kangra district, lies north of Kulu, east of Chamba, and south of Rupshu, which is Kashmir territory.

Lahoul once had the reputation of holding good ibex and red bear, but in 1911 I could neither see nor hear of the former, except a few unshootable beasts, right up by Parseo and Kailing (not Kailang), around the Baralacha pass. Red bear, of which there are still a few left, seem to have been shot down by the same merciless hands which have almost exterminated them in Kulu. There are bharal near Lingti Sarchu and in the Tsarap valley, while *Ovis ammon* occasionally visit the latter country; but I was unable to discover at what time of year they usually come. The shepherds grazing there in 1911 knew nothing about them. On the whole, Lahoul is a poor sporting country.

5. Spiti is the next country on the east. It is bare and inhospitable, and holds nothing but bharal and a very occasional ammon ; a very few ibex worth shooting.

6. The Sutlej valley seems very poorly supplied with game. There are tahr and goural, red bear and black bear scattered about, but none of these are plentiful enough to be worth making a trip after them. Higher up there is good bharal ground, while *Ovis ammon* are plentiful across the Tibetan border, which may not be crossed without a Lhassa permit, practically impossible to obtain. The right bank of the Sutlej is the limit of the ibex.

7. Kumaon, Gahrwal and Tehri Gahrwal. This brings us to a much better sporting country. Tahr, goural and serow are plentiful, while good bharal are easily obtainable a few marches from Naini Tal or Almora. Near the Tibetan border *Ovis ammon* and yak are occasionally to be got. Sambhar penetrate right up into the hills near Naini Tal, and are there called " jarao ". Transport difficulties are now considerable, however, and have rendered these districts difficult of access.

This brings us to the native states of Nepal and Bhutan, which are forbidden ground to the sportsman.

Chitral is virtually a preserve for the local garrison. It holds ibex, markhor, oorial and leopard ; also a few red bear. A man stationed in Chitral has a better chance of bagging a snow leopard than in any other place, except perhaps Gilgit, which is also always a reserve for the officers in that station.

Having decided what you want to shoot and where to go for it, the route to the ground is the next consideration. Those to Naini Tal, Almora and Mussoori are to be found in the railway guide-books, and they are all within a few hours of railhead.

The onward routes are best dictated by the most recent local information available on arrival at one of these places.

To get to Chamba, Kulu, Lahoul or Spiti, rail to Pathankot. Thence by tonga or dooli to Dalhousie, and on by pack transport 22 miles to Chamba. For Kulu, motor to Palampur (there is a railway now being built up the Kangra valley which should be open in 1928), and thence by pack transport, six marches, to Sultanpur, the chief town. Lahoul and Spiti are both reached from Kulu via the Rotang pass, which is usually open in the second week in May.

Neve's *Tourist's Guide to Kashmir, etc.*, is invaluable to any one making a trip anywhere north of the Sutlej.

The main road to Kashmir is from Rawalpindi via Murree, to Srinagar by motor, a total distance of 196 miles. It is a very fine road, and there are good dak bungalows at regular distances along it, where halts may be made and meals obtained. It is best not to attempt to drive the whole distance in one day, as the curves are decidedly dangerous. Motors may be hired from a dozen different firms in Rawalpindi. There is an alternative route by Hawelian and Abbottabad, joining the Murree route at Domel: the total distance from Hawelian to Srinagar is 169 miles.

There are two routes to Kashmir through Poonch, both passing through Poonch town. One is from Sihala station on the N.W. Railway, by pack transport through Kahuta and Panjar, crossing the Jhelum by bridge at Lachman Patan, and thence by Palangi, a total of six marches to Poonch. The other route is eight marches up the Poonch river via the famous fishing centre of Tangrot, to Poonch town, and is popular with anglers. It is rather a rough track. From Poonch town, the traveller can then cross into Kashmir via the Haji Pir pass, which joins the Murree route, 50 miles from Srinagar, at Uri (four marches); or cross the Pir Panjal pass and march a total of seven marches from Poonch town to Srinagar.

There are two routes from Jammu, both via Udaipur over a low pass to the Chenab valley. One a motor road, then goes on to Srinagar via the Banihal pass, a total of 163 miles; the other, a bad track, goes up the left bank of the Chenab eleven marches to Kishtwar from Jammu, and is not to be recommended. There is always much trouble about coolis, and the track is broken up by avalanches and mud-slides early in the year. Both routes are very hot after May.

If travelling up by motor from Rawalpindi, send the heavy kit on by lorry with a servant if possible. A lorry will take three or four days.

SHIKARIS.—In Kashmir and Chamba all shikaris are registered and licensed by the state. In other hill countries they will have to be picked up locally as you go along.

When going to Kashmir, find out if possible the name of a good shikari from some sportsman who has been up there recently; then write ahead to engage him either through one of the several agencies which exist in Srinagar, or through the Secretary, Game Preservation Department, Srinagar. The same procedure may also be adopted if no shikari is known, but it is essential to mention what particular species of game are wanted, or which district is to be visited, as each shikari has his own particular beat, and is not much good away from it.

Chamba is so small that the average shikari obtained in Chamba town will know most of the nullahs.

In Kashmir and Chamba the shikari will bring along a tiffin cooli and three or four permanent coolis. It is best to take the men he recommends, as it helps to ensure harmony in camp. The sportsman's own servant should do the cooking: it will save his pocket, and he is not so liable to leave him in the lurch if he finds the trip too long or cold for his liking.

It is particularly necessary in Kashmir to see personally to the paying of all coolis and local men, and to make sure that the permanent shikari and his coolis do not live at the expense of the villagers to their sahib's loss. The average Balti or Ladakhi is very easily bullied, and the Kashmiri shikari or camp cooli is an expert at extracting food and milk without payment. The very best of Kashmiri shikaris are bullies and swindlers, and they are withal so plausible that the new-comer is apt to take a liking to them and refuse to believe in their guilt. Never trust a Kashmiri; he has no motive but self-interest.

A Kashmiri shikari is a very efficient specimen of his class. He manages a camp well, makes a study of the best localities, and is often a good stalker and judge of heads, but it must be remembered that he is out for money, and if he thinks he can get as much out of a sportsman by making him comfortable, flattering him, and showing him shootable (but not really good) heads at an easy distance from Srinagar, he will invariably do so.

The Chamba shikari is not nearly such a knowledgeable man as his confrère of Kashmir. He confines himself to the production of a camp and tiffin coolis and directing the sportsman to a nullah. Arrived there he will probably show little stalking ability, but will know the likeliest places for finding game, and will almost certainly turn out to be an excellent climber. The Kashmiri shikari does not shine in really bad ground, and is easily outdistanced by both Baltis and Kishtwaris. I have found a Kashmiri tiffin cooli and a camp cooli belonging to an officer marching ahead of me, weeping bitterly and almost paralysed with funk, on what is known as the "old road" between Lidraree and Atholi in Kishtwar. This has to be traversed early in the year, for parts of the new road are almost always carried away by spring avalanches. The "old road" is difficult for loaded coolis, but is, of course, nothing to the ground over which tahr are hunted. A Kashmiri will often decline to cross a rope bridge without assistance.

Expense.—The following is an approximate table of monthly expenditure in Kashmir :

	Wages.	*Ration Money.*
Shikari	Rs.30 0 0	Rs.5 0 0
Tiffin cooli	12 0 0	4 0 0
4 Camp coolis @ Rs.10 . . .	40 0 0	12 0 0
Personal servants 2, @ Rs.25 . .	50 0 0	10 0 0
	Rs.132 0 0	Rs.31 0 0
15 Marches, 16 coolis @ 6 as. . .	240 0 0	
Stores	50 0 0	
Supplies	50 0 0	
Local shikari, 15 days @ 8 as.. .	7 8 0	
Bakshish and sundries . . .	30 0 0	
Total . .	Rs.509 8 0	
Add ration money	31 0 0	
	Rs.540 8 0	

A Ladakhi Shikari.

To face page 34.

The journey to and from Rawalpindi and Srinagar will cost about Rs.400, including the days spent at Srinagar in the hotel or boat, and cost of heavy luggage.

At Srinagar the following articles will have to be purchased :

5 leather yakdans @ Rs.8	Rs.40	0	0
1 tiffin basket	1	8	0
1 khud stick	2	0	0
3 pairs chaplis	10	8	0
4 pairs leather socks	2	0	0
For wear with grass shoes } 6 pairs puttoo socks, outer	8	0	0
For wear with grass shoes } 6 pairs woollen socks, inner	6	0	0
For coolis, 20 pairs snow-goggles	4	0	0
For shikari and camp cooli, 8 pairs chaplis	16	0	0
For shikari and tiffin cooli, puttoo socks, 6 pairs	8	0	0
For shikari and tiffin cooli, inner socks, 4 pairs	6	0	0
	Rs.107	0	0

A Balaclava cap and gloves of pushmina are also useful.

Then it is customary to give the shikari about Rs.10 for a suit of clothes, and he and the tiffin cooli must be given a blanket each.

The monthly expenditure has been calculated on a fairly liberal scale, but I think that the total cost of a three months' trip to and from Rawalpindi may be roughly assessed as follows :

3 months at Rs.500	Rs.1500	0	0
Journey to and from Rawalpindi	400	0	0
Initial expenditure in Srinagar	150	0	0
	Rs.2050	0	0

With a longer trip cost of the journey, licence, initial outfit will be spread over a greater number of months.

THE RIFLE

THE question of the selection of a rifle for big game shooting is one on which there is a very great difference of opinion amongst hunters, and arouses the most acrimonious discussion. That experts can differ to such an extent shows that any individual advice can only be taken as the outcome of personal experience and not as exclusive of rifles not recommended, so the following notes must be read as such.

The *laudator temporis acti* brought up in the school of great Nimrods such as Baker, Oswald and Gordon Cumming, and scornful of the scientific application of principles of weight of bullet and velocity, vehemently asserts the necessity of a large bore and heavy bullet. He is usually ignorant or negligent of the fact that equally great hunters such as Selous, Sharpe and Neumann discarded these cumbrous weapons for the lighter and more powerful cordite rifles of smaller bore and lighter bullet, but absolutely efficient in accuracy, penetration and smashing power.

All the three last-named giants of the chase went further than most men are prepared to go nowadays in the search for lightness and accuracy, in using a ·303 for elephant shooting, a proceeding justified in their cases by their wonderful knowledge of how, when and where to shoot and place their bullet.

Since their active days of hunting, further developments have taken place in the manufacture of sporting rifles, inaugurated by the Ross ·280 with its 3000 feet muzzle velocity, which has since given rise to a host of imitators, utterly eclipsing the old small bores such as the ·275 Mauser and ·303 Lee-Enfield.

This group of small bore rifles with muzzle velocities ranging from 2400 to 3000 feet per second may be classed as "magnum" small bores.

In discussing the selection of a rifle no attention will be

paid to obsolete black powder rifles such as the ·500 and ·577 expresses, and I shall refer to but two of the small bore (non-magnums), the ·256 Mannlicher and ·303 Lee-Enfield, for purposes of comparison only.

The actual bore only affects the efficiency of a rifle when combined with a suitable velocity and weight of bullet, to produce accuracy and, above all, killing power; which latter may be paraphrased as "striking energy".

"Striking energy" at any given range is determined by the weight of a bullet and its remaining velocity.

In stating "killing power" and "striking energy" to be synonymous, it is postulated, of course, that the right kind of bullet is used, and that neither (1) is the energy wasted by a solid bullet driving clean through an animal, making a small wound and expending most of its power on the air beyond; nor (2) is the power all expended by using a soft bullet for, *e.g.* the head shot at an elephant, whereby it mushrooms out on the bone and penetrates no vital part.

Thus in selecting our rifle the principles that guide us are: (1) that it should be thoroughly accurate up to and slightly beyond the range at which it is most frequently to be used, and (2) that it should have sufficient striking energy at that range to kill outright with a well-placed bullet, and so severely wound with a body hit as to make the beast's escape to die a lingering death a strong improbability.

Now, as a general principle, it can safely be asserted that the larger your beast the thicker the country it will live in, and consequently, the closer your shot. Then the larger the bore of the rifle, the greater its killing power, but the higher its trajectory and the shorter the range up to which its accuracy can be relied on. For heavy game living in thick jungle your rifle need not be built to shoot with extreme accuracy at ranges over 150 yards, as most shots will be taken at a much shorter distance, and the rifle is built accordingly, accuracy at long range being sacrificed to increased killing power at close range.

But in the hills and open plains shots will usually be at over 150 yards and the animals smaller, so that a flat trajectory is essential and killing power may be reduced.

Let us consider thick jungle and heavy beasts first.

The shot is to be at 80 to 100 yards as a rule, and a knock-down blow is wanted. At first it appears as if the sportsman had better take along the heaviest rifle on the market. But why waste unnecessary energy. Even a ·450-·400 (*i.e.* a rifle of ·400 bore and ·450 chamber giving increased velocity and shock) will suffice to kill any beast in the jungle, and the ·425 of greater velocity and striking energy is even more efficient.

Increase of bore means increase of weight, and by the time an old bull bison has been followed for several hours in hot weather and through thick jungle, every ounce of weight will tell. If you do not carry your rifle yourself you deserve to lose your shot (and probably will), and if you do none of the tracking yourself you lose all the real sport of the chase, and reduce it to a long walk with live target practice at the end of it if you are lucky. I speak of tracking as being the highest form of jungle shooting, and one which the real sportsman is bound to take up sooner or later.

Therefore, say I, if you are going after big game such as bison, tsine or elephant, take a ·450-·400, or a ·425 by a well-known maker. Have it double-barrelled, hammerless, ejector, of simple action, and the best you can afford.

Now for hill shooting. There is little to choose between the ·280 Ross and a ·318 Axite for the hills. There are many other small bore magnums, but none of them seem to meet the case as well as the above two rifles.

At ordinary sporting ranges (and further in the case of the ·280) they produce those extraordinary results on game, known as "explosive" effects, owing to the shattering of the tissue for several inches round the wound, thus producing a sort of tunnel of blackened coagulated blood and pulp. These effects have never been satisfactorily explained.

In May 1912 I inaugurated a long correspondence in the *Field* on the subject, but most of the many correspondents strayed very far from the point, and none would account for these explosive effects being produced by a ·280 bullet at 400 yards and not by a ·303 at 80, the latter having the greater remaining velocity.

These "explosive effects" of the magnum small bores of

course enhance their efficiency enormously, and as they do not seem to be produced by any rifle of less than 2400 feet muzzle velocity, the older small bores such as the ·256 Mannlicher and ·303 have been quite outclassed.

It is a curious fact in support of the view that velocity has a great tendency to increase killing power in a degree not calculable in arithmetical values of striking energy, that the ·256 Mannlicher, which had the highest velocity of all the old small bores up to the appearance of the ·280 Ross, was much the most effective of them on game, despite the fact that its lighter bullet gave it, arithmetically, a striking energy at 180 yards very slightly different to that of the ·303 ; which to me, after a long experience of it and several others, seemed to be only surpassed in inefficiency by the ·375 Mannlicher-Steyr.

To return to the selection of rifles. I have said that I prefer the ·280 Ross or ·318 Axite (Westley Richards) for the hills ; for their lightness, handiness, flat trajectory and killing power combine to make them unsurpassable for work in the Himalayas and kindred countries.

We have now arrived at selecting two rifles for specific forms of shooting ; and, assuming a sufficient balance at the bank, a ·425 D.B. h'less ejector and a ·318 D.B. or magazine are to be bought.

Now comes the vexed question of the balance at the bank.

At least three men in four who go after big game in India are far from wealthy, and it is quite possible that a ·425 rifle costing not less than £60 will be too much for their pocket, particularly if they propose shooting in the hills as well, to which it is not at all suited.

These men will be looking round for the best "all-round" rifle. Now let me say at once, that a thoroughly efficient all-round rifle does not exist.

But many a poor man would like to follow the finest of all sports within the limits of his purse, and I had to begin that way myself.

I began in the Nilgiris with an old black powder ·500 express, then went on to a ·303 in the U.P. ; then successively to a ·275 Mauser, ·375 Mannlicher-Steyr, ·355 Mannlicher-Schonauer (a beautiful weapon, but with a sudden drop in trajectory after

180 yards), and finally a D.B. high-velocity ·475 h'less and a ·280 Ross. In the intervals I tried a ·256 Mannlicher and a ·360 Gibb, and all the time I retained a ·303 in reserve (the cartridges being so easily obtainable) until I got my ·280 Ross and the big double rifle. I made these changes through saving money and getting a bit back by selling the old ones. Having for eight years to tackle all varieties of game with light (and cheap) rifles I had to learn very carefully where to place my bullet, and the psychological moment for pressing the trigger. The result was that I found that when I went into heavy jungle that I could do as good work with the ·280 as with the ·475, and accordingly discarded the latter on account of its weight, and bought a second ·280.

With the first of these during four years in India, Burma and Somaliland (in eighteen consecutive months of which I was only out for a fortnight), I killed 125 head of 42 species of big game, including the following varieties: tiger, leopard, bison, tsine, sambhar, greater kudu, warthog, oryx, *Ovis ammon*, red and black bear, ibex, markhor, Kashmir stag and tahr. Surely a fairly representative list.

In 1911, during six months' actual shooting in the Himalayas, I fired at thirty-nine beasts, missed two (both running shots), lost two black bears with a smashed thigh each due to snapshots in thick jungle (the one drowning in a snow-covered river, the other getting into a deep cave), and brought the remaining thirty-five beasts to bag, including seven bears.

Now all this speaks volumes for the ·280 Ross, especially as a rifle for use in the hills; but nevertheless it must be remembered that I had had a thorough good grounding before I bought it, and had done more, and more various, big game shooting than most men succeed in putting in in ten years, unless they are professionals.

The fact remains that I do not recommend a novice to start shooting in thick stuff with a ·280 Ross; and, in fact, to use a ·318 Axite in preference to it, and strongly advise him to use neither if he can afford a heavier rifle.

I have now two ·318's, and they undoubtedly have greater killing power at short ranges than the ·280 against such heavy beasts as the bison and tsine, and from October

1919 to July 1923 I killed, with 65 cartridges, 44 animals of 14 species, including bison and tiger, with my first ·318.

So, if you are a man of moderate means, want to shoot in both hills and plains and must confine yourself to one rifle, get a ·318 Axite.

Shooting Record of ·318 Rifle of Lt.-Col. C. H. S. Stockley

Date.	Range.	Shots Fired.	Animal.	Result.
7/10/19	200	1	Kashmir stag	Miss. Fired standing.
9/10/19	150	1	Do.	Kill. Base of neck.
Do.	180	2	Do.	Kill. 2nd shot unnecessary.
12/10/19	200	3	Do.	Kill. 1st broke shoulder, 2nd missed, 3rd kill.
25/10/19	50	2	A brown bear and a black bear	Killed right and left.
26/10/19	70	1	Brown bear	Kill.
10/11/19	200	1	Oorial	Killed. Heart.
21/11/19	300	1	Do.	Kill. Spine smashed behind shoulders.
30/11/19	200	1	Blackbuck	Miss.
1/12/19	220	1	Do.	Kill. Heart.
10/12/19	160	2	Sind ibex	Kill. 1st miss, 2nd chest.
11/12/19	180, 240	3	2 Sind ibex	Both killed.
22/2/20	90	1	Bison	Kill. Base neck.
23/2/20	50	1	Barking Deer	Running. Killed.
1/4/20	120	1	Do.	Kill. Heart.
11/4/20	40	1	Bison	Kill. Heart. A very big bull.
1/5/20	35	1	Tiger	Got away very badly hit, found three days later dead.
11/5/20	170	1	Thamin	Kill.
13/5/20	180	2	Do.	Kill. 1st shot missed.
23/10/20	70, 140	2	2 Oorial.	Both killed.
Dec./20	Av. 160	5	5 Oorial	All killed.
3/3/21	130	1	Blackbuck	Killed.
10/3/21	120, 140	2	2 Chinkara	Both killed.
12/3/21	180	3	Chinkara	1st broke shoulder, 2nd missed, 3rd heart.
10/7/21	70	1	Panther	Kill.
14/7/21	200	1	Chinkara	Kill.
16/7/21	160, 180	2	Oorial	1st body wound, 2nd heart.
18/7/21	170	1	Chinkara	Kill.
10/10/21	120, 160	2	2 Sind ibex	Both killed.
24/12/21	160 to 40	4	Chinkara	Hit too far back and had to be tracked up.
12/10/22	80	1	Kashmir stag	Miss. Head only visible, and shot taken standing.
19/10/22	160	2	Do.	1st broke shoulder and entered chest, 2nd at 5 yds.
27/10/22	150	3	Serow	Killed.
April/23	Av. 150	6	5 Chital	Killed. One needed a 2nd bullet.
July/23	140	2	Chital.	Kill.

Totals: 65 shots fired and 44 animals killed.

It will be noticed that I have said little about soft-skinned dangerous game such as tiger and leopard. These are easily killed with any of the weapons I have mentioned, and an *expanding* bullet—capped or copper-pointed, not split. But the ideal weapon for them is a ball and shot gun such as the Paradox or Explora. These are light and handy, accurate and hard-hitting at short ranges, but without great penetration. It would be folly to go after bison or tsine with one, but they are just the thing for tiger and leopard.

I have said nothing about medium bores such as the ·350 and ·375 magnums, as they seem to me to combine the deficiencies of both small and large bores with the advantages of neither. A man using them will have to learn his business just as carefully as when using a ·318 if he intends taking on heavy, dangerous game; and for the hill shooting they are heavier and have a higher trajectory.

The question of magazine or double barrel is a difficult one, and largely a matter of personal preference. Many men cannot shoot effectively (especially at a moving target) with a single barrel, and consequently stick to a double, both with small and large bores. The magazine gives the advantage of several shots in rapid succession, while the first two can be fired quicker from a double-barrel. The slight difference in time may be of value in very thick stuff, but the magazine rifle will often save much trouble with a wounded beast in the hills, and there is not the same risk of being left to face a dangerous wounded animal with an empty rifle, as may well happen with only two shots at one's disposal.

The magazine rifle has the advantage of cheapness, but I do not believe in the heavy magazine rifles of ·400 or larger bore now on the market, in lieu of a double of the same bore. These very heavy magazine rifles are unsuitable for use in the hills, and the weight of a double ·425 is not beyond any man's strength.

To sum up. If you are going to shoot exclusively in the plains and jungle, get a ·400 or ·425 double; if in the hills, a ·280 or ·318. If your means do not run to two rifles, and you intend shooting in both hills and plains, get a ·318.

But—and a big but—novices should not go into heavy jungle after dangerous game with a light magazine rifle.

The ways in which they may come to grief are too numerous. A shot may be badly placed through ignorance of the meaning of the beast's movements, and consequent hurry in the mistaken idea that a change of position means he is going to bolt; through impatience; through excitement when coming on him suddenly at short range in thick forest; through failure to take into consideration the angle at which he is standing. All these are errors to which the novice is liable, and then there is a wounded beast going off to die a lingering death; or, perhaps, he is overtaken, and a charge is met by a shot at the wrong moment hitting the wrong spot, and—another regrettable accident is chronicled in the obituary column of the papers.

All these errors, or the liability to commit them, can be eliminated by experience and experience only. Therefore, if you have to use a light rifle for all-round shooting, first take two or three trips after blackbuck, oorial, ibex, and such like animals, which will teach you to keep cool and hold straight.

The errors of the novice shooting dangerous game in thick jungle will be largely discounted by a heavy bullet and high velocity at short ranges. The shock of a wound from such a rifle, if the hit be anywhere in the body, is very much greater than from a small bore. A flesh wound at the first shot with either bore will make the animal clear off altogether, and a broken limb will render him almost harmless. The body shot is the one to consider, and the experienced man's careful selection of the right spot for a disabling shot, due to his knowledge of anatomy and the amount of time he has at his disposal to await a favourable opportunity, is the result of many days after game and the actual visible effects of previous shots. This knowledge is not to be acquired through books, and it is it which renders a Selous with a ·303 more than the equal, at 50 yards from a buffalo, of Jones the novice with a double-barrel cordite ·577, even though Jones be a Bisley winner.

Little has been said about stopping charges; for there again the man behind the gun is so much the dominating factor in the argument, that it is impossible to take the matter largely into consideration in buying a rifle.

The careful, knowledgeable man of experience so rarely gets into a bad mess that he hardly thinks of the matter; and, when the danger comes along, it is infinitely more his coolness and straight shooting that turns or stops the oncoming bulk, and a field-gun will not save a novice without straight shooting.

One last word about "striking energy". Do not be satisfied, when buying a rifle, with the gunmaker's statement of muzzle velocity and energy only. If the bullet is not suitable, both in shape and weight, to the bore of the rifle and the velocity at which it is despatched, it will lose velocity, striking energy and accuracy very rapidly and often very suddenly. The ballistics of a rifle may be entirely satisfactory to 150 yards and much the reverse at 200. Therefore, ask your gunmaker for a statement of velocity and striking energy at 50, 100, 150 and 200 yards, and also for a trajectory table up to the same ranges, giving the rise of the bullet above the line of sight, and the drop below it, for possible errors in sighting.

Sight your rifle with a wide V back-sight, having a small silver line under its centre.

The fore-sight should be of the caterpillar, ivory or platinum bead type.

A Lyman aperture sight is liked by some men, but they are easily damaged and need much practice.

A telescopic sight may be useful in bad light, but it is easily knocked out of adjustment and rather an encumbrance in the bush. It is an unnecessary adjunct for any man with normally good eyesight.

Have the rifle sighted for 75 yards for jungle and 150 yards for hill work, and see that the flap sights have good springs so that they will not easily be raised by accident.

For the hills a rifle should be fitted with a sling.

Carry a spare fore-sight, a spare sight protector, and plenty of oil and flannelette for cleaning.

Keep two cleaning rods; one with a cutting-screw end for removing broken pull-through cords.

Never use a worn cord, and, if you have not an absolutely trustworthy man to do the cleaning for you, clean the rifle yourself; otherwise there will inevitably be a broken pull-through stuck in the barrel one day, and a consequent expenditure of time and temper in extracting it, with possible damage to the rifle.

Boiling water is the best thing for cleaning barrels and loosening fouling, followed by plentiful cleaning with alternate dry and well-oiled rags, and ending with a slightly oiled rag. The B.S.A. preparation, "Cunirid" paste, is excellent for removing metallic fouling.

Paraffin and coconut oil are useful for removing fouling, but should never be left in the barrel.

A rifle is worth the very greatest care that you can give it; grows to be a friend, the feel of which gives pleasure and confidence; and when a well-liked weapon is parted with it is like losing a trusted helper.

This explains why men are so keen in defence of a favourite weapon, and uphold its merits so staunchly against other bores and makes.

If you have a rifle you do not trust, get rid of it.

Give every rifle you buy a fair trial, and get to know it well, and when you find one to suit you, stick to it till you or it are both worn out and no longer fit for the great game.

OUTFIT

HAVING selected a shooting-ground and purchased a rifle, there still remains the camp outfit and stores to be considered.

These will of course vary with climate, and inquiries should be made as to the quantity and nature of local supplies available. For instance, in Burma the villagers do not milk their cows, and all milk must be taken in tins. Fruit and fresh vegetables are almost unobtainable in some districts, so that dried or tinned substitutes must be carried. Eggs are very scarce in Hindu districts in the hills, and unobtainable in the Rupshu district of Ladak.

The following lists have been compiled as general guides, and not to be rigidly followed:

CAMP KIT AND EQUIPMENT

80 lb. tent with bathroom. (The poles must be jointed.)
2 small servants' tents.
Table, chair, bed and bath.
Iron pegs.

Rifle.
Gun.
Cartridges.
Field-glasses.
Telescope. (Hills only.)
Camp pocket-knife.
Rifle oil.
Flannelette.
Belt with shackle and cartridge pouches.

Camera and films.
Pencils, diary, letter paper and stamps.

Six yakdans. (These should not be too big or exceed 50 lb. when full.
Valise and bedding.
100 ft. of rope for tying loads.
Housewife, containing needles, thread, etc.
Maps.

Medicines. (Quinine, chlorodyne, cascara, salts, permanganate of potash, borofax, boracic powder, vaseline, lint and bandages.)

Axe.
Hurricane lamps.
Petrol tin for kerosene oil.
Long nails for pegging out skins.
Skinning knives.
Preservative.

Cooking Pots, etc.

A set of four aluminium nested degchis.
1 frying-pan.
1 kettle.
1 chopper.
1 kitchen knife.
1 do. spoon.
1 board for cutting up meat, etc.

2 double hot-water plates. (Hills only.)
2 soup plates.
2 large plates.
2 small plates.
1 cup and saucer.
1 teapot.
1 milk jug.

Screw-top receptacles for salt and pepper.
2 table knives.
2 small knives.
3 forks.
3 dessert spoons.
3 teaspoons.
Tin-opener and corkscrew.

Clothes, Bedding and Toilet Requisites

1 macintosh.
2 coats of shikar cloth } Substitute two puttoo suits for the hills.
2 prs. khaki shorts }
2 prs. puttis.
4 khaki flannel shirts.
1 pr. khaki or grey flannel trousers.
1 woollen cardigan.
2 old tennis shirts, for evening wear in camp.
1 scarf.
2 sleeping-suits.
8 prs. thick woollen socks.
12 handkerchiefs, preferably khaki.
3 bath towels.

1 pr. nailed shooting-boots.
2 prs. canvas stalking-boots. (Chaplis are the thing for dry weather, but useless in wet.)
1 pr. old tennis shoes for camp use.
1 pr. slippers.
1 cork topi, khaki.
1 puttoo hat.
Spare bootlaces.
Tooth paste.
Shaving soap.
Bath soap.
3 packets Sunlight soap.
1 doz. jharans.

Bedding

Blankets according to climate.
A wadded quilt (razai) for the hills.
A mosquito net.
A pillow.
2 prs. sheets for the plains, but not needed in the hills.

Add for the Hills

1 greatcoat.
4 thick Jaeger vests.
4 do. do. pants.
1 pr. warm gloves.
Dark goggles for snow or glare. (Essential.)
1 khud stick.

STORES FOR TWO MONTHS FOR ONE

Flour, 15 lb.
Jam, 10 lb.
Paisley flour, 4 lb.
Dripping, 6 lb.
Tea, 4 lb.
Sugar, 20 lb.
Milk. According to district. If in Burma, 1 small tin per diem.
Soup squares, 1 doz.
Cornflour, 2 lb.
Quaker oats, 4 lb.
Macaroni, 1 lb.
Butter, 8 lb. (In many districts in the hills good butter is obtainable locally.)
Curry powder, ½ lb.
Salt, 2 lb.
Pepper, ¼ lb.
Mustard, ¼ lb.
Bromo, 2 pkts.

The above are all essentials, while the following may be taken according to transport available and the taste of the sportsman, local possibilities (*e.g.* in the matter of fruit and vegetables) also being considered. It should always be remembered that it is false economy to cut one's food supply unnecessarily :

Cheese.
Cocoa.
Chocolate. Almost essential.
Dried fruit. Essential if fresh and not locally available.
Sardines. For lunch.
Army ration. The Maconochie takes a lot of beating, if bivouacking for the night.
Biscuits. Cream crackers are a very good substitute for bread.
Candles. A reserve in case of accidents.
Raisins and currants. For cakes or puddings.

A 2-gallon tin of kerosene oil should be carried, a petrol tin being the most suitable.

In hot weather lime juice and sparklet syphon are invaluable.
Once again, do not stint the food.

A tarpaulin may be substituted for a tent in forest countries where there is plenty of shade, especially in the dry season.

A gun may be taken or not, according to the likelihood of it paying for its keep in the way of filling the pot.

With regard to clothes, shorts are not liked by every one, but I strongly advise that flannel be adhered to, and cotton wear eschewed : it leads to chills and tummy troubles.

I would also advise the addition of a butterfly net and the two *Fauna of India* volumes on butterflies. They can be caught on the march or in camp, pinched and kept in envelopes. They form an interesting study when halted, and can be relaxed and set on return to civilisation.

Of books I have said nothing. Some few are essential, and I strongly recommend that one be *Whitaker's Almanac*, while the *Pioneer* to keep one in touch with the world at large, and the *Field* for good reading value, are most useful additions and should be ordered before starting.

"Mars" oil for one's boots, and a Primus stove are very useful luxuries.

Consider what transport is to be used, and pack the baggage accordingly. It is a sound principle to pack all one's kit in 50-lb. loads, so that cooli transport can be used at any time if necessary. Leather-covered yakdans are useful anywhere.

The best size is 28 inches by 15 inches by 10 inches. They can be best purchased in Peshawar, Rawalpindi or Srinagar.

All packages should go under the seat of a railway carriage, and be suitable for pack transport.

Avoid small packages which have to be carried by hand (the hurricane lantern and bath-water tin are unavoidable) and label everything clearly. Labels can be printed cheaply in any Indian bazaar.

Last, but by no means least, carry plenty of cash and small change. Notes are little use in the jungle, and individual payments of small amounts is much appreciated, instead of a rupee having to be shared out by two or three.

MARCHING AND CAMPING

Before departing for a shooting trip it is a good thing to send all heavy kit in advance to the point of departure from the railway; it is especially useful if a competent servant or orderly can be sent with it. He can then arrange transport for the next stage, and it is as well to tell him to try and get hold of a lorry if possible. Many small places in India now hold lorries, and, though not beautiful to look at, they may save some days' marching.

When travelling by rail it is advisable to see one's luggage from one brake to the other at every change; otherwise it is probable that it will arrive a day or two late at the other end.

Watch the kit stowed in lorries or carts. The Indian has a trick of loading the lighter and more easily damaged articles first, then dumping heavy stuff on top of them. He will also pile everything up in a top-heavy pyramid, so that the first bump brings them crashing down.

When you change to pack animals or coolis do not overload. It never pays in the end. Keep with the transport in bad going and give a helping hand. Take top loads off animals in crossing really bad bits. I once lost a pony-load of trophies through neglecting this precaution.

Before starting in the morning cooli loads should be distributed as evenly as possible, and an extra anna or two promised to the carrier of the heaviest loads. Do not let your underlings bully the coolis.

Personally I do not believe in long marches. They are, of course, occasionally unavoidable, owing to the absence of a suitable intermediate halting-place; but a series of forced marches destroys the pleasure of a trip, and, if carried out before the traveller has got really fit, he will be knocked up by over-exertion. If carried out with pack transport, galls and break-downs will occur. Yaks, for instance, will simply lie down and decline to proceed further if marched too far on consecutive days. This may lead to a very awkward situation.

It is very annoying to be held up by weather, but local advice must be taken as to the feasibility of crossing a pass with much fresh snow on it, or in threatening weather; or, again, traversing a cliff dangerous from falling stones after heavy rain. It is not fair to override their advice and risk their lives, just because you are in a hurry to get to your shooting-ground. Similarly, get up early in the morning when about to cross a snow pass. Avalanches come down late in the day from the sun loosening the snow, and though you may be in camp by then the coolis may still be struggling along with 40-lb. loads, and get caught.

Camels are almost helpless on muddy ground, and usually end by falling and breaking a leg if pushed.

It is inadvisable to go too fast or get far ahead of the transport. In case of an accident or unforeseen delay, there is no one to take charge, and being stranded miles ahead of the food and kit on a cold or wet night is not enjoyable. The best principle is to see the baggage off, then walk or ride on ahead to half-way. Have lunch and wait for the kit; then push on again to the halting-place and select the camping ground and arrange for supplies and the next day's transport.

Do not try and walk too fast; you are probably carrying nothing and your shikari or tiffin cooli is loaded with rifle, field-glasses, camera and food. They will only be tired out and no use to you when you get to camp.

CAMPING.—If possible, select a site for the camp at a sufficient distance from a village to avoid smell, flies and pi-dogs. The last are an absolute curse at times, not only on account of their howling at night, but because they are inveterate thieves, and to see one going off with a prized trophy is too infuriating for words.

In a hot country shade and breeze are governing factors in siting a camp; in the hills, shelter from the wind is often essential if the tents are to remain standing.

A good water-supply within easy reach is also necessary.

"Zho's" Yak-oxen half-breeds. Ladakh.

A rope-bridge over the Chenab. Nanny the milch-goat crosses.

To face page 52.

In every case see that there is no chance of the tents being flooded out by rain, and dig a good trench round each tent, just inside the inner fly, to carry off rain-water.

Before actually pitching the tents, cut some branches or make a broom of grass, and, after cutting down any vegetation on the site, sweep it thoroughly, so that no cover remains for snakes, scorpions or other noxious vermin.

Pitch the tents with regard to the sun and prevailing wind, according as to whether warmth or cool is wanted. Also see that the cook's fire is not so placed that all the smoke drifts into your tent.

See that the tent-pegs are a good distance from the flies, so that the walls stand straight upright, and not at a slant; it is extraordinary how much the room in a tent may be increased by proper pitching.

SUPPLIES.—On arrival send at once for the headman of the village and order what supplies are needed; such as eggs, milk, fowls and wood. Also give orders for the supply of transport for the next march.

Be careful to deal fairly with the local people. Remember that they are very poor and sometimes *cannot* supply what you need, however much you pay; while work in the fields, which is their livelihood, makes the provision of transport often very difficult.

Do not put down all failures to get what you want to ill-will on their part, and, above all, see that they are properly paid for what they supply, and that your own retinue do not impose on them. It is better (while carefully avoiding extravagance which may reflect badly on others) to slightly overpay rather than risk leaving discontent behind, through failure to satisfy a perfectly just claim.

Obstacles to travelling must be expected in wild countries, and should be tackled reasonably and without petulance or bad temper.

HEALTH.—The first thing to be thought of in the East under the heading of health is the question of water-supply.

In the *higher* hills an absolutely safe water-supply is usually obtainable from a mountain stream at the tent door; but everywhere else, where there are villages near by or higher up towards its source, it is essential to have one's water boiled before drinking, and this should be seen to personally.

Camp filters are little good, as they foul very quickly. A lump of alum moved about in a bucket of muddy water will precipitate the dirt.

"Chaguls", or canvas water-bags, are invaluable for keeping water cool in hot weather, and for carrying it on the shooting-ground when a supply is wanted for a whole day or longer. The water in them freezes easily if used in mountain bivouacs.

As far as food is concerned, do yourself well, and try and see that it is properly cooked. A camp cookery book is of great assistance. Avoid fat in hot weather, and be particular to eat fresh or dried fruit daily. In very cold weather most people experience a craving for sweets, and I have found a stock of butter-scotch just the thing on many a bitter day on the Tibetan border.

The question of alcohol is largely a matter of taste. Personally, I give it up in the hills, but like a peg before and after dinner in the plains. A sparklet bottle is a great improvement to the outfit. A small bottle of champagne is a marvellous reviver if absolutely tired out, and a few should be brought if possible. A bottle of brandy must always be carried for medicinal purposes.

Tackle any illness, however slight, at once, and do not try and carry on shooting when ill. Not only will it very likely lead to serious trouble and spoil the rest of your leave, but you will probably miss every shot. It is only sensible to take a rest in camp, and start again fresh. On a long trip I always take one day in camp every week, to go through my skins, check stores and generally spring-clean.

Use a mosquito net always in malarial country, and take 10 grains of quinine on two consecutive days every week to keep fever away.

In the case of wounds from a dangerous animal, clean them immediately and thoroughly with an antiseptic, and get qualified medical aid as soon as possible.

There will be constant calls made on the medicine chest by villagers. Many of these are made with a view to securing a free dose to be saved up against eventualities; some are by

An ideal camp on the Kashmir-Chamba border.

Snowed up in April at 7,000 ft. Kaj-i-Nag.

To face page 54.

sufferers from incurable diseases, and some are genuine cases to be treated at discretion. It is impossible to help all, and it is better to keep one's assistance for those who immediately serve you, temporarily or permanently. A few grains of permanganate in water and the simple faith of the applicant often do wonders. Hot water and cleanliness will heal wounds in the bodies of these simple livers in an amazing way.

The best advice to remember is, keep fit in order to keep fit. The man who does not stint his food unnecessarily, overtax his powers of endurance, or take unwise chances with his health, will keep fit and enjoy every minute of his shoot.

SEARCHING FOR GAME

To find the particular kind of beast you want to shoot, and one (in the case of a horned animal) which carries a trophy worth having, a knowledge of the habits of your quarry is essential.

Before setting out to shoot, study the mode of life of the animal in whatever literature is available; then, having obtained reliable information as to a district in which they are sufficiently plentiful, secure a licence (if necessary), and go there at the season which is favourable for hunting.

This last point should be very carefully ascertained, for it is useless to go after a beast which is to be hunted by tracking at a time when the ground is iron hard and covered six inches deep in dry leaves. Then the terrific downpour of the monsoon will render hunting quite useless in some districts, for tracks are washed out almost as soon as made, and the undergrowth is so thick as to render it impossible to see your quarry at over ten yards distance.

Having reached your district, the first thing to consider are the feeding habits of the animals you are after. They will be found, or sufficient indications of their presence, wherever food is most plentiful. Now, every animal is much easier to find and approach when it is feeding than when it is lying down. The hunter must therefore be on his ground by the time the game commences feeding and commence his search either for the beast itself or its tracks as early as possible in the day. Tracking is fully treated in another chapter, and hill game and still hunting will only be dealt with here.

Firstly, hill game.

Start out in time to reach a point commanding a wide view of the feeding-grounds, then settle down in as comfortable a position as possible, and get out the field-glasses and telescope.

It will usually be found that the native shikari is not much good at using a telescope, though often quite an adept with the field-glasses; occasionally he is much better without either.

In any case use the telescope yourself, unless he is better than you with it.

There are two usual positions for using a telescope for searching.

One is sitting (on a rock or downhill slope) with the telescope pressed against the khud stick with one hand, the elbow on the knee. The other hand holds the eye-piece of the telescope. Steady the khud stick against the inside of the knee. The khud stick may be then moved so that the field of the glass travels slowly over the opposite hill-side, a change of elevation being made by shifting the glass a little up or down the stick at the end of each traverse.

For the other method, some sort of rest to pillow the head is essential, and the position is only used to search ground on a higher level than the hunter.

Lie flat on the back with a stone or other rest under the head, raise one knee by bending the leg, and cross the other leg over it. Then press the telescope against the outside of the thigh by resting the wrist on it. Traverse the glass by moving the leg.

Work the glass slowly, thoroughly searching the best bits.

The first individual seen of a herd will probably be a female, and the old males will usually be slightly apart. Quite often an old male will be lying down while the others feed, and be quite hard to make out in the shadow of a rock or tree perhaps forty yards distant from the main body of the herd.

I remember one day in Eastern Kashmir spending over an hour watching half a dozen barasingh hinds before I found the stag, although I was certain the cunning old brute was there somewhere (for I had seen him the day before), and then all I could see was the top half of a horn sticking out from behind the trunk of a fallen pine tree, and looking at first very like a broken bough.

In still hunting and close country a telescope is a useless encumbrance and the eye will be used unaided for searching, the field-glasses only coming into action after a beast has been spotted, either to make out the rest of the herd, or to ascertain if the head is a good one.

In the hills a telescope is absolutely essential. Most beasts are spotted a mile or more away, and field-glasses are not sufficiently powerful to make out the size of the heads at such a distance, while it may be a matter of several hours climbing to get to a point within effective view of the herd.

Having spotted a shootable beast, a decision must be come to as to the best way to get in an effective shot. In still hunting it will usually be a mere matter of waiting till he shows clear and at a favourable angle; or, at most, of a short stalk. In the hills, however, one of several reasons may make it inadvisable to carry out the stalk that day. The ground may be too unfavourable, the wind shifty, the time involved too great, or a storm impending. With beasts such as ibex and markhor, it is nearly always worth while watching them for a day to ascertain their feeding habits, and their resting-place. Then an early start may be made, often in the dark (perhaps from an over-night bivouac), which brings the hunter early in the morning to a point favourable for a stalk, and with the whole day before him in which to carry it out.

In close country and thick forest, sharp watch should be kept for movement. All the hunter is likely to see at first is a quick whisk of a tail, or a six-inch patch of brown hide move past an opening in the branches. "Monarchs of the glen" clear cut against the sky-line are not to be found in India. At least I have never seen one. A stag sneaking along the hillside with head low and horns laid back, is a most inconspicuous object, and when feeding he usually seems to have a tree between you and him. If he crosses the sky-line at all he will not waste time about it as a rule, but choose the spot that will give him a little cover right up to the last moment.

Sheep and goats will often be seen on the sky-line, but with many pairs of eyes on the watch from the most commanding positions, and the small bands of very old males which retire in late summer into small ravines high up in the mountains have a wonderful way of picking out a bit of ground to feed or rest in, almost completely hidden yet commanding a wide view.

Deserted Temples in the Jungle; now the homes of Bear, Panther and Deer.

To face page 58.

These places are only to be found by a careful consideration of the quarry's habits.

Food, water and safety from disturbance or enemies are the considerations which govern a beast's choice of sojourning-place. His natural enemies, other than man, will not make him move very far as a rule, and in some cases (oorial for instance) will live close to man, and even mix with the flocks or cattle on occasions. But food a beast must have regularly; and water too, though not nearly so often as people think. Consequently find out where food is plentiful and the ground undisturbed, and there will your old males be. They will travel several miles for a drink which will take them as many minutes to swallow, but it takes them hours to fill their bellies with grass.

To sum up, in order to find your animal you must study his likes and dislikes, and when you know a district to hold good heads of the species of game you are after, and you can find nothing but females and immature males, apply the science of deduction to discover the whereabouts of the old males, and do not just tramp blindly over the hills. They must be somewhere, and a few days' careful searching are certain to bring success. Above all, in all searching and still hunting do not go too fast. Work ground thoroughly and not hastily. If you go too fast you will make much noise, expose yourself to view too frequently, and jump your beasts. Lying quiet on a hill-side or moving soundlessly through the jungle, skirting the open spaces with every sense on the alert, and you will see and hear instead of being seen and heard.

THE STALK

By a stalk is meant the approach to within range after the game is sighted. It is consequently an art that does not come much into play in heavy jungle, its place being taken by either the superior art of tracking or the much inferior one of beating. It often happens, of course, that in tracking the hunter will sight his animal sufficiently far off for a short stalk to be made to bring him within shot, but the principal exercise of the craft is in the hills and open plain country.

In stalking the eyes and nose of your beast are your enemies throughout the stalk, the ears only in the latter stages.

First of all guard against being seen. Wear clothes to match the ground, not whole-coloured, such as plain khaki, but of mixed shades varying from dark grey to greenish-brown. Your shirt, collar and hat should be of the same inconspicuous shade, and as far as the latter is concerned, I would strongly recommend a dark grey "Curzon" topi in the hills in preference to a khaki "tent club" pattern. The latter is apt to bleach, and, though suitable for the plains, is too big, and presents at close range a blot of colour unlike anything usually to be found on a Himalayan hill-side, where the dark-grey "Curzon", especially if a little travel-stained, closely resembles a bit of rock.

The stalker's handkerchief should be of neutral tint and preferably of silk. A large silk handkerchief fits easily into the pocket, lasts a longer time, and is strong enough to be very useful for odd jobs on occasions.

Let us assume that the beast to be stalked is an ibex, an animal which is usually found in ground practicable nearly everywhere.

The herd may be seen either the same day as it is stalked

or the day before, but in either case the object of the stalk is to reach a spot within range of them. This spot may overlook the place where they are actually seen lying down or feeding at the time of stalking, or only the place where the stalker expects to find them. In any case, the first thing to consider in selecting the desired spot is the wind. Now nearly all game keep a sharp watch below and on both sides but seldom look uphill, consequently that is the direction from which the approach should be made if possible. The wind will always blow uphill during about nine hours of any sunny day; will blow downhill in the early morning and late evening, and is nearly always variable and untrustworthy on a very cloudy day. In any case the uphill wind is the one most to be trusted, and the spot selected for the shot should consequently be uphill of (not straight above) the beast stalked, and the stalker should so time his arrival there that the wind has commenced blowing uphill. The place for the shot should not be too near (130 to 160 yards is about right), or on showing his head from under cover he will probably be seen, and the herd bolt immediately. If he shows his head at about 140 yards he is quite close enough for accurate shooting; is less likely to be spotted; and, even if some of the herd catch sight of his head, they will almost certainly stand and stare long enough for him to get in a steady shot, knowing that they are safe from a snow leopard at that range, which beast is the enemy that will probably enter their heads at first.

The stalker has now got as far as selecting a spot for his shot about 150 yards from and slightly uphill of the herd, and the next thing is to set about getting there.

It is extraordinary how small a bush or tuft of grass will suffice to hide a man if properly used, and another point to remember is that as long as he keeps still, a beast will often be deceived into thinking him part of the landscape.

Bearing both these points in mind and taking care to keep below the sky-line, it will be hard if, having started say half a mile from the herd, the stalker cannot reach an intervening gully and use its shelter and that of its offshoots to bring him nearer to his firing-point. Up to about 400 yards (or closer if a strong wind is blowing) he need take few precautions about noise, but after that it is necessary to keep in mind that, although few beasts will pay more than passing attention to the sound of falling stones, unless too frequent in recurrence, the crack of a breaking stick will instantly put them on the alert, and probably cause them to move off. If surprised during a stalk by the herd changing position or feeding into sight, freeze solid and stay frozen. They may come into easy shot or move off; but in the latter case, unless they cross the wind and so are warned, they will be there again for a shot another day; whereas the least movement and they are certain to catch sight of the stalker, and that will be the last seen of them for a week or more in all probability. If cramp compels movement to ease a limb, it must be slow and gradual, so that it may not attract attention. If the herd feed over the sky-line, wait a little after the last has disappeared before going on, for one or two will often come back to have a last gaze.

During the stalk test the wind frequently with a bit of fluff plucked from the coat, or some fine dust.

On getting close to the firing-point have a good rest, to recover breath and steady the hand, before actually coming up to sight the herd. Have glasses and cartridges handy, pick your head carefully, and mark down the next best head if he is worth shooting.

Unless the shikari is of use in judging heads, leave him behind out of sight of the herd.

A stalk in the plains is no different in principle to one in the hills, and varies very little in the actual carrying out, except that it may involve a large amount of crawling snakewise to gain a desired bit of cover. The same caution as to breaking sticks is needed, and the same device of keeping absolutely still is employed in the case of being surprised when out of range.

The usual causes of failure in stalking, other than actual errors by the stalker, are, other beasts (such as pheasants, or an outlying young male of the herd) suddenly starting up and making off in sight of the quarry, or sudden changes of wind. Neither can be guarded against, and in the first case the only thing to do is to stay quiet, and in the second to go home.

These sudden changes of wind are very frequent and annoying when hunting *Ovis ammon* in Ladakh. The great rounded bare hills and numerous glaciers make it very unreliable.

There is one thing to be said about hats. The sola topi makes a horrid scratching noise if a branch rubs against it, but the light " Curzon " is not stout enough to guard against a hot-weather sun, and is of unsuitable colour. A thin puggri cloth cover is often a useful thing to avoid noise. For the rains a cork khaki-coloured " Ellwood " is the right kind of head-gear. A Cawnpore tent club sola topi becomes a mere mushy ruin in heavy tropical rain.

TRACKING

TRACKING is to other forms of big game shooting what dry-fly fishing on the Test is to other fishing. It is the fine art of the sport, from the picking out of the right pair of tracks to the final shot which secures the trophy.

The following hints are written with a view to following game and achieving the final result by tracking, but are mostly applicable also to the marking down of a beast with a view to beating.

No man will make a success of tracking unless he studies the habits of his quarry so thoroughly as to know when he is approaching a likely spot, and can distinguish and draw inferences from jungle noises. He must also study particularly carefully where to place his shot, for a miss will very seldom be followed by a second chance, and a wound may mean disaster to himself.

Now in tracking, " all things must be done decently and in order ", the order being as follows :

First, find your tracks.

To do this it is not necessary to plunge into the thickest jungle. Having secured the best available native assistance, arrive at the feeding-grounds at sunrise or before, and move carefully along the jungle paths, the *edges* of clearings, and the open tops of ridges. Keep your eyes open for other signs in addition to footprints, for an overturned ant-hill or young tree reduced to kindlings is almost as frequent a sign of an old bull bison or a stag.

Having found tracks, the next thing is to determine to what species they belong. That is only to be done (1) by reference to your native helpers ; (2) by experience ; (3) by carrying copies of the tracks shown portrayed on such a sheet as the one which accompanies this chapter. Having deter-

TRACKS OF HOOFED ANIMAL.

Walking

Tracks in pairs. No earth thrown forward from toes. Carry on.

Trotting

Tracks evenly spaced. Some earth thrown forward from toes. Halt. He will turn and look back every now and then. Give him 15 minutes then follow carefully and slowly until he walks again.

Cantering

Tracks arranged 3 and 1. Much earth thrown forward from toes. Carry on until he trots, or else give up; according to time of day. He will go some distance.

To face page 64.

mined the species, the sex and age can be decided in the same way. The track of the forefoot of an old male ungulate (hoofed animal) is always blunter at the toe, squarer and broader than that of the young male or female. The track of the forefoot (not the hind) is always sufficient to determine the species, age and sex of the animal which made it ; and, with a little experience, an imprint of the front third of the foot will be sufficient to give all necessary information. The heavier the bull the more deeply will the track be indented at the toe.

The diameter of the track of an elephant's forefoot multiplied by $6\frac{2}{7}$ gives twice its circumference, equal to his height at the shoulder. This will prove correct within a couple of inches.

Having found the track of an old male, the next thing to determine is its age, which is to be known by many different signs, mostly dependent on the time of year, the weather, and the nature of the soil.

Dry heat will dry loose mud soil or droppings, discolour sap, and wither bruised grass and fallen leaves, much quicker than damp heat ; while in cool, damp weather the changes are very slow.

If the track is well marked, examine the loose soil at the toe and edges. When fresh it is soft and of the same colour as the soil inside the track, and dries lighter in colour. The next sign is insects inside a track. These work a little fine, loose earth down in the corners of a track. A worm-cast or well-formed spider's web deep down in a track are signs that it is worthless to take up. But a light spider's web is sometimes spun across the top of a track in the very early morning within two or three hours of the animal's passing. If the track is in dust on hard soil or in deep sand, the age may be told by the amount of blurring at the edges, the ridge left by the cleft of the hoof being a particularly good guide.

If there has been rain lately, the time of the last fall is a sure guide to the age of the tracks, which will show whether made before or after it. A light shower is very useful on dusty ground, for the inside of tracks will show and retain hard clots of dust for a long time.

All the above indications apply to the actual footprint, but as a rule there are many additional evidences from which may be deduced the time that has elapsed since the animal passed.

The principal of these are the animal's droppings.

Droppings of all deer and antelope, sheep and goats, are in the form of pellets, the size being according to that of the beast. They vary in shape according to which of the above four tribes the animal may belong, but all will show by their degree of moistness and friability, how long they may have lain since deposition. If very fresh there will be a little whitish mucus on some, and sometimes a few may be found adhering together by this means. Owing to their small size and shape, they do not retain warmth for long.

The ordure of the cattle tribe is deposited in large masses which retain warmth up to half an hour after evacuation, and dry slowly, their age being thus fairly easily ascertainable up to as much as twenty-four hours, and sometimes later. The cattle tribe will often, when travelling, drop large pellets which dry rapidly and are hard to age accurately, but it is an almost invariable rule that they will evacuate a large mass before and after lying down between feeds.

Elephant droppings are large-formed lumps (shaped much like those of a horse) which usually contain little moisture, though this varies to a certain extent on the nature of their food and the season.

The ordure of the carnivora is much like that of the domestic dog, and is usually black, though that of the hyæna dries into a very hard white substance.

Bears' droppings are usually very soft and contain a lot of undigested matter, showing on what they are feeding, and hence they are often an excellent guide to where the animal is most likely to be found.

Other points in ageing a track are :

Moist earth kicked forward from a footprint dries from the front back to the toe.

When a stone has been kicked out and there are still insects in the hollow, the animal has passed very recently.

If urine still retains bubbles, the animal has passed within the last half-hour.

When the track crosses a stream the water in the holes

left by the feet should be examined to see if it is clouded. With slow-running water mud will sometimes continue to drift away from the footprints for half an hour, but in absolutely still, shallow water it will usually settle in less time, unless the animal has stood about in it.

Both bison and tsine are fond of knocking down ant-hills with their horns. The ants immediately start walling up the galleries thus broken open, and the material used in repairing is moist and much darker than the rest of the mound. An ant-hill thus broken down is of the greatest assistance in fixing the time of the bull's wanton effort, as the amount of work done by the ants shows up very clearly, and if the work has been completed (1½ hours to 2 hours is usually sufficient for the worst breaks), then the colour of the repairing material will show the extent to which it has dried. Occasionally a bull will leave a very clear print of his horn on an ant-hill.

Little can be written to aid the sportsman in making deductions from broken boughs, bruised grass and leaves. The discoloration and withering are so dependent on the temperature and humidity of the atmosphere, and on the particular species of vegetation involved, accurate information is really only to be obtained by experience.

When walking on a clear track look as far ahead as possible, not at the footprints immediately at your feet. Footprints make a shadow and are often more conspicuous three or four yards ahead than at closer range, while the eyes are better focussed to catch movement further ahead, a sudden change of direction in the tracks, or perhaps some unpleasant obstacle, such as a snake, lying in the way.

In following up a blood trail, the following points are useful to remember:

(1) If the blood is flung in splashes diagonally away from the trail, the wound is in a leg.

(2) If the blood is very bright red and (sometimes) with bubbles in it, it is in the lungs.

(3) If the blood is thin and mixed with watery fluid, it is from the bowels.

(4) Blood from a large vein or artery is plentiful, and of a clearer red than that of a mere superficial wound.

(5) If a hind foot has trodden blood, the wound is well forward.

(6) If in passing through bushes the blood is mostly on the under side of the leaves, it is far back and high up.

(7) A broken leg is indicated by long scratches made by the trailing foot.

When looking for tracks, do not allow the natives with you to waste time by hovering over old and worthless tracks to discuss the size and movements of the beast that made them. Get on to tracks as early as possible, so as to catch the animal feeding. It is infinitely easier to get up to your animal feeding than when he has lain down for the day. All animals select their resting-places with great care, and most of them so as to command a view back on their own trail.

It is often well worth while taking up tracks twelve hours, and sometimes even twenty-four hours, old. For an animal is not actually walking away in front of one, and a mile to a mile and a half an hour, is about the limit of the pace at which he will feed. An animal must fill his belly or starve, and naturally he prefers to take his time about it; the bigger the beast the longer being the time required for the process. When on old tracks move as fast as possible. An animal will usually feed over much the same ground for several days before changing to another track, and his trail will constantly return and recross itself, so that corners are cut to an extent that makes it often less than an hour's work to puzzle out a period of four or five hours' feeding. Then the lying-down place is reached, accounting for another five or six hours of the animal's time, and the hunter is then within measurable distance of his quarry. Care must always be taken to keep a good look out ahead to avoid running into an animal which has returned and is lying down on its tracks. If the beast is jumped in this way at fairly close quarters, it is often well worth while sprinting hard after it, as an old bull bison or tsine will usually crash off for sixty or seventy yards not going faster than a man can run, and then stop and turn round for a short stare; or, if he does not actually stop, will usually moderate his pace to a fast walk. It is especially worth while running after your beast in at all broken country, as you may

TRACKS OF INDIAN BIG GAME. ABOUT $\frac{1}{4}$ NATURAL SIZE (EXCEPT BEAR $\frac{1}{8}$).

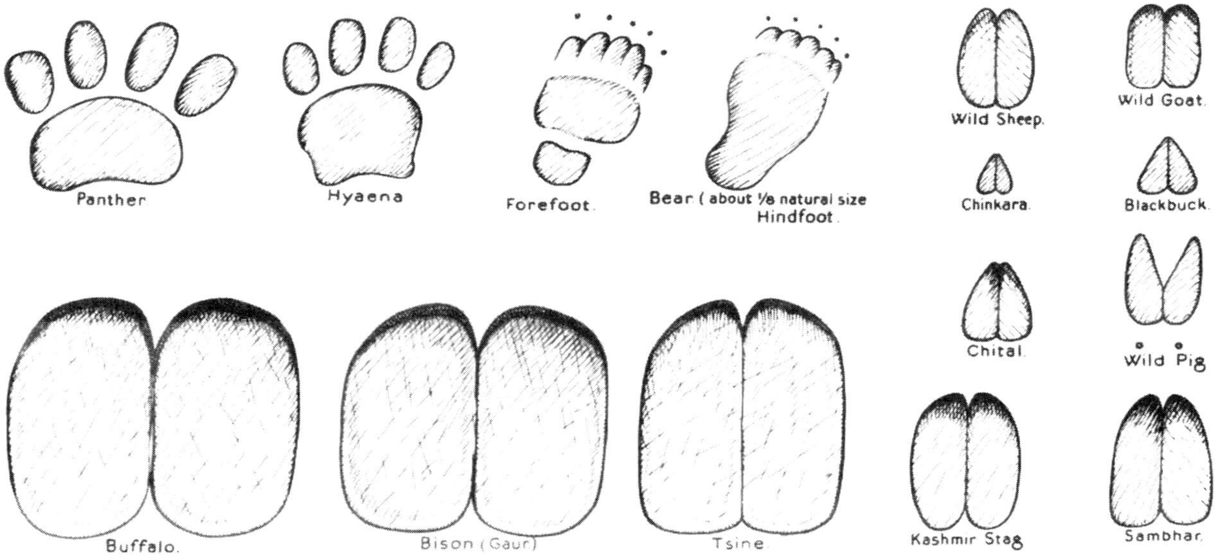

Note.—The characteristics of each animal's track have been emphasised. Individual animals vary to some extent so that after hunting the same species for some time, such individual differences are recognisable even by the European. The trackers of the Lower Indus Valley will carry the track of an individual camel through those of a hundred others. The forefoot tracks of old male hoofed animals are given. The tracks of hind feet are smaller and more pointed, and resemble the tracks of females and young males.

To face page 68.

get a shot into the broad of his back as he climbs the opposite side of a nullah within quite comfortable range.

Risks must be taken when moving on fresh tracks or the hunter will not overtake his quarry, and he will be very unfortunate indeed if he does not meet with some sign to tell him that the animal is near.

Keep your native tracker close to you, and do not let him forge ahead and come into sight of the beast while you are twenty yards or more behind. Five yards is the limit that he should be ahead (except when making a cast to pick up a lost trail), and when on very fresh tracks he should be within reach of a touch. If taking no part in the tracking yourself, look ahead and avoid hindering the tracker.

All the above is written merely as a very sketchy guide to tracking. It is a science that cannot be learnt from books, and experience is the great teacher.

Any white man who has a love for the woods and takes the trouble to apply the science of deduction to what he sees, can reach a degree of proficiency not usually attained by the average village shikari; and although he can never hope to rival the professional trackers of such tribes as the Bhils or Gonds, yet even with them he may take a minor part while following a trail, and in Burma he will have the pleasure of doing the whole job himself. Then in the Himalayas and other Northern Indian hills, the art of tracking is largely neglected, and the sportsman who knows something of it will find it of the greatest assistance in helping him to discover the whereabouts of game.

On sitting down to rest or have lunch, pluck some leaves, break a small branch, bruise some grass blades, muddy a stream or break open an ant-hill; then time the changes that occur, and write them in a note-book. Do this repeatedly, and in a week the knowledge gained will be surprising, and as time goes on the whole jungle will become amazingly interesting, and more pleasure derived from it and its inhabitants than in any other form of sport.

There is no trophy I am so proud of as the head of the big bull taine which I followed up and shot without the slightest assistance from any one; and I only hope that what I have written may help some others to experience an equal pleasure.

BEATING

I PUT beating well below tracking and stalking as a method for big game shooting, in the matter of providing real sport.

I do not mean to infer that it is not a scientific method of bringing game to bag, but that to any but those stationed in forest country, it is so hard to acquire the necessary knowledge to plan and carry out a beat, that it is usually left entirely to the local shikari, the gun merely letting off his rifle at the beast which has been brought within range of him by no knowledge or exertion of his own.

Beating carried out in this fashion is not a very high form of sport, though affording plenty of fun and amusement in pleasant surroundings. Quite four-fifths of the beats made in India are done in this way, and there are many whose reputations as hunters of dangerous big game have been obtained wholly through the knowledge and hard work of their native helpers.

Nevertheless it is a very interesting form of sport, and those who plan their own beats usually become skilled hunters and observers; if they do not, they meet with small success.

It is therefore necessary before planning a beat to know a good deal about the habits of the species to be driven, and very often of the individual animal.

The first thing to remember is to try and drive the beast in the direction in which it will naturally be most inclined to go. It is no use trying to force animals into wide open spaces from thick cover, or downhill when they want to go up. It will only end in their breaking back, sometimes with serious damage to a beater. Even sambhar have occasionally been known to kill a man when breaking back.

Having decided on the line of the beat, the next thing is the placing of the gun or guns. It is almost always advisable to post them high up in machans, on rocks, or astride the branch of a tree. This is not so much on the score of danger, but to get a clear view from above the undergrowth, and because the game is less likely to see a man when he is above it.

There are many patterns of machans, from the rough cane seat or sawn-down kitchen chair, to the elaborate padded affair, with cupboards for lunch and drinks, which is to be found at the shoots of native potentates or other great ones of the land. Whatever post is taken up for the gun, it should allow a view of the animal's probable line of approach, with a 45 degree swing for the gun from square opposite to that amount of angle *past* his post.

No shot should be fired towards the beaters, or in the case of a dangerous animal, until it has passed the line of guns. A beater may be hit, or a wounded beast be sent back into the beat, where it will sometimes go straight back and break out, killing or wounding some defenceless unfortunate on its way. I have known a tiger go a hundred yards with a bullet tear through its heart.

Having decided on the positions for the guns, the stops must then be posted. These should be carefully selected, and their method of turning an approaching animal towards the guns be fully explained to them; such points as whether they are to tap continuously or only on seeing the animal, or cough, or break branches, being emphasised. They should be taken to a central gun position and sent outwards to their posts from there, just before the beat begins.

The method of beating will also depend on circumstances. It may be decided to have a "silent" beat, which is carried out with fewer coolis, who pass slowly through the jungle in line, occasionally tapping a tree or carrying on a low-voiced conversation. This method is usually more successful with horned game, or with an animal which has not fed heavily. The noisy beat is carried out with a large number of coolis (according to the size of the jungle to be driven), reinforced by tom-toms, kerosene oil tins, and other instruments for producing noise. The silent beat will often not shift a determined beast, or he may lie low until the line is quite near, and then bound back suddenly through it, but few animals will face the terrible din of a noisy beat, if unwounded. It is no use trying a noisy beat with too few beaters: the absence of noise at any particular spot will tell an animal just where to break through. With a silent beat it will often think that it is merely being disturbed by a party of woodcutters, and walk quietly up to the guns.

The object of the beat in every case, is to bring the animal past the guns at a pace which will ensure an easy shot.

Quiet is essential on the part of the guns. Movement catches the eye and warns the microphone-like ears of the quarry. It may be lying up quite close at the beginning of the beat, and hearing the guns shifting about or talking, slip back past a stop. A hand flicking away flies may give away the position, and the beast lie up in a thick patch and bolt back through the line, rather than face it.

The instinct of a hunted animal for the real point of danger is often almost uncanny.

In beats, as at all other times, it is a rule that wounded animals must be followed up. It is an unpleasant job in the case of a dangerous animal, and only the foolhardy and inexperienced can possibly take any pleasure in it. The following up must be done with the greatest care, men being sent up trees commanding the line of approach, and thick patches stoned from under cover. Go slow and keep an even pace. Above all do not get careless after the first half-hour. A panther or tiger can hide in very little, and I once very nearly put my foot on a panther for which I was searching in grass not 18 inches high. Fortunately for me he was unwounded, and bolted.

Give every beater a token before starting. An old pack of cards dealt round is very good; they are then paid on producing their cards at the end of the day. If this precaution is not taken it will be found that extra men will turn up for payment who have no claim, and they may be paid at the expense of the rightful workers.

A system of signals should be arranged with the beaters to indicate the result of a shot. An agreed number of blasts on a whistle, or red or white flags may be used; the red flag to indicate a wounded or doubtful beast, the white a clean miss or kill. A whistle should always be carried by which to halt the beat in the case of an animal going back wounded into it.

Much more might be written on the subject of beating, but space forbids. I would recommend those who want to study it further to read *Big Game Shooting in India, Burma and Somaliland*, by Col. V. M. Stockley (the author's uncle), and that very instructive book, Dunbar Brander's *Wild Animals in Central India.*

SITTING UP

Sitting up at night is the last method which should be employed in hunting big game. It has the very great disadvantage that a shot is never certain, and an animal is often sent away wounded. By the aid of electric light or similar help, the actual chances of a clean kill may be greatly improved; but there is little enough trial of the hunter's skill or endurance in any case, and the adoption of such artificial means is repugnant to most. It would appear, however, that if sitting up is to be done at all, any means which will ensure a clean kill, and minimise the chances of undue suffering to the animal, are to be recommended.

No sitting up should ever be done for a large animal such as a bison; there is little chance of a fatal shot, and a great one of a stomach wound, by which the beast will never be brought to bag.

It is a very necessary method in some cases, however, and in particular with tiger and leopard in countries where they cannot be driven, *e.g.* the Sunderbunds and parts of Burma. Any method may be adopted which will help to destroy that nasty beast, the leopard.

In the case of man-eaters, either tigers or leopards, sitting up has almost invariably to be done.

Method.—The first bit of advice which I would give, is to avoid using a machan and sit on the ground whenever possible, if after tiger or leopard. Their sense of smell is almost nil, while their eyesight is excellent and hearing extremely fine. As they almost always circle round the kill or bait before coming on to feed, they catch sight of the sportsman against the sky, or hear him. There is perhaps a more probable chance of the latter, for another trick is to wait a few yards away in a clump of bushes or other cover, and there listen. A creak of the machan, which is never comfortable, or a rustling of the leaves, and the chance of a shot is over for the night.

Sit on the ground inside a small hedge of thorns or bamboos, with the branches cut into sharp points so as to form a *chevaux de frise*. Have a small porthole made, with a thick bar at the bottom on which to rest the rifle, and at a suitable height for firing from a sitting position. The kill or bait should be about three yards from the porthole.

This is comfortable, and consequently the man inside will not be continually shifting his position, as is almost invariably occurring in the case of a machan being used.

If possible build the shelter so that the back can be rested against the trunk of a big tree.

It is quite allowable to go to sleep, unless given to snoring, and a string tied from the kill to the ankle will give warning of it being moved.

On the arrival of the quarry, all that is necessary is to sit up, level the rifle (which should be left with the muzzle through the loophole, resting against the lower bar), and press the trigger. A shot at such short range and on the same level should almost certainly score. A 12-bore gun loaded with bullet or large slugs is a very efficient weapon for this game.

Nearly all my sitting up has been done for leopard which have become a destructive nuisance, and I have had two chances for every blank. I have been told by men who have done a great deal of it, that one chance in thirty attempts is a good average for sitting up in machans.

To show how poor is a leopard's sense of smell, the following may be of interest.

I was sitting up for a brute which had been destroying the milch goats of my detachment in Somaliland. He came back once to the kill just before sunset, but was frightened off by some passers-by. About 10 P.M. he came again, and I heard a little gravel dislodged a few yards below my shelter, which was built of branches and large stones on the side of a hill, the kill being level with me.

The leopard came up behind me, walked up round the back of the shelter, and coming up to its left side began rubbing himself backward and forward against the shelter, making a sort of internal rumbling, which was the nearest thing to a domestic cat's purr I have ever heard from a wild animal. He was about 18 inches from my left shoulder, and my rifle was thrust out through the loophole, ready for him to get on to the kill in front of me: I could not withdraw it or he would have heard me. The shelter, of course, had not been constructed with a view to standing this sort of treatment, and suddenly it gave way and the leopard's hind quarters came in with it. I was sprawling on my back, with a large stone on my tummy, and he actually shoved off from my thigh with one foot to regain his position. There was a Somali in with me who was carrying a large knife in a wooden sheath, and I heard the rattle of this as he drew it, and was expecting it in my ribs at any moment. A wild yell from me sent the leopard off, and I expect he was just as frightened as me, which is saying a good deal; and I was left swearing at the Somali, to try and cover up the fact that I was feeling decidedly shaken and rather a fool.

If tying up for a man-eater or in very open ground, a pit may be dug and roofed in with stout branches or beams, an aperture about six inches high being left in the direction of the kill or bait. This aperture may be carried the length of that face, if necessary.

The bait or kill must be very securely fastened to a post or heavy log by a stout rope. A leopard can easily pick up a goat in its stride without the slightest difficulty. I once saw a leopard jump nine feet up on to the top of a rock with a full-grown female oorial in its mouth, which it had just killed, and it did not even crouch for the spring, but made it without the slightest preliminary effort.

Whatever you sit up in, have it made comfortable. Discomfort leads to movement, which is fatal.

Occupy the position a couple of hours before sunset. A tiger or leopard often returns to its kill while the sun is sinking, or at dusk.

A very fatal and comfortable way of sitting up by day may be practised in the plains. Very often low rocky hills crop up near jungle villages, and these are almost certain to hold a panther or two. If one is located, occupy a position about four in the afternoon, which commands the route by which the village goats are driven home. Instruct the goatherd carefully to have one goat ready with a rope round its neck, and to fasten this to a bush below you as he passes.

The goat will bleat loudly when it sees its companions disappear, and will probably draw the panther in a very short time. The leopard may be seen sometimes before it gets near the goat, and shot with ease. If it does not arrive by dusk, walk down, undo the goat, and go home to camp and dinner, of course seeing to the safe onward course of the bait.

THE SHOT

To prepare yourself for taking shots at big game it is absolutely necessary to have considerable previous practice with the actual rifle to be used. This practice should be carried out not only at bull's-eye targets on a range but at unfamiliar objects, such as earthen chattis, at unknown ranges, from 50 to 200 yards in ground which makes judging distance necessary, and the objects fired at moderately difficult to define.

Having arrived at a useful degree of proficiency at such objects, the tyro may then go forth with a fair hope of killing (not wounding) a blackbuck or other animal; but before taking on the larger and rarer animals, or starting on a regular shooting trip of two or more months' duration, it is distinctly advisable to make a maiden essay at such game as blackbuck or chinkara. These teach a sufficiency of self-control and patience, without overtaxing the stalker's ability or offering too difficult shots.

The first thing to consider before taking your shot is the range at which you are firing, and the usual judging distance rules are as follows :

Bad light . . . . . Flat ground . . . . A background giving poor definition . . .	All make the range look longer.
Clear light . . . . . Across a valley or water . Clear definition against a contrasting background .	Make the range look closer.

These rules are for animals approximately on the same level as the sportsman, but when firing up or down hill (particularly the latter) the sight should always be taken low.

THE TOP OF A HIMALAYAN PASS.

A BROWN BEAR AND A BLACK BEAR.
Shot right and left. Shamshibri Mts.

To face page 87.

The tendency is always to overshoot, and it is a good principle to knock 15 per cent off every range as judged.

Up to 200 yards may be termed ordinary sporting range, but it is strongly recommended that the tyro should carefully pace all ranges where practicable after firing, and I think he will find (and many experienced men also) that the range which he judged to be 200 yards is more often than not only 160.

In judging the range the height of your beast at the shoulder should be previously known, and his apparent size is then a very helpful guide to accurate shooting.

A goural, for instance, is only 27 inches at the shoulder, and is a remarkably small target at any range over 80 yards, especially as a hit must be scored in the vital organs.

See the bead of your fore-sight clear of the back-sight, take your time, and squeeze the trigger; don't pull or jerk it.

Then reload quickly, watch your opportunity for a second shot at another good head if the first is dead; but do not fire wildly if you have missed, or empty your magazine at the retreating herd. If you do, an unshootable little buck or wretched doe will be the most likely victim, and you the object of thoroughly well-deserved jeers and obloquy from older hands at the game.

If your beast is alone and falls to the shot, reload before going up to it; but if it is going off wounded, shoot at it steadily and quietly as long as it is in possible range.

The selection of a point to be aimed at is largely governed by the angle at which the beast is standing. With all except elephant, the shooting of which is treated separately in the chapter devoted to them, the heart shot is the one to be tried. The front edge of the heart is to be preferred, for if there is a slight error forward the shot will break up the big blood-vessels of the chest and be equally effective. A raking shot from either end is effective with bison and tsine, the root of the tail and the small hollow in the chest just below the throat being the points to aim at.

THE "HALAL".—Before going on to consider the actual skinning of the head the question of the "halal" must be disposed of.

In any country or district where Mohammedan shikaris are employed, they will want to cut the throat of all edible game while there still remains a spark of life, in order to render it lawful food according to their religion. This is called making it "halal", and unless this is done the meat is useless to a Mohammedan.

Where they have been getting a regular supply of meat it is easy to forbid this being done in the case of specimens of which the skin or mask is wanted for mounting; but, in the case where meat is scarce, it is obviously undesirable to do this; while in the case of wild tribes whose only object in coming with the sportsman is to obtain meat, any arbitrary deprivation thereof may lead to an entire cessation of local assistance, which is often quite indispensable.

It is, however, possible to induce many Mohammedan shikaris to "halal" an animal so low down that the cut does not affect the head-skin, though of course damaging to an entire skin wanted for mounting. If the entire skin is wanted for mounting, it is probably better to have the "halal" made right in between the angle of the jaw-bones. In any case the cut should be kept as small as possible, often a difficult matter with a wild jungly excited by the sight of so much meat. Often the cut made low down will not be accepted as a proper "halal", particularly with the more ignorant; but it has been found possible to induce such people to make a longitudinal cut starting between the jaw-bones and then, turning back the skin, to perform the "halal" under it. This sounds difficult, but is in reality very simple, as the skin of the throat can be pushed back with the hand.

It is often very trying to find on reaching the animal that the shikari has rushed ahead and cut its throat all round from ear to ear.

Materials for Skinning.—To skin a large animal four good knives are needed. The Army and Navy Stores sell a good set of four; but good knives are easily bought in any bazaar, those used by mochis being particularly suitable.

A hone or sharpening stone is also needed. An oil-stone in a wooden case is the best.

For pegging out a skin 6-inch wire nails are the best. About 200 should be carried.

Skinning and Preserving Masks and Flat Skins

Let it be assumed that the sportsman has shot an animal carrying a trophy rather above the average, and of which he wants to preserve the mask for mounting.

Sketch.—If he has a little talent in that line, a sketch of the head and neck, particularly of the profile and of the shape of the eyes and nostrils, is particularly valuable.

Photographs.—These are of great value. They should be taken from two or three different angles—profile, full-face, and oblique.

Colouring of Soft Parts.—Note the colours of the eyes, eyelids, nose and lips. A dab of water-colour corresponding to each on a slip of paper is most helpful. Note the shape of the pupil, whether round or oval, and whether clear-edged or blurred. Also note the ground colour of the skin in any parts likely to fade.

Measurement of Horns.—This for the sportsman's own information. "Horns" includes both hollow horns and antlers.

Antlers:

Length.—Should be measured from the base of the burr over the curve, following the back of the horn, to the tip of the longest tine.

Girth.—Taken midway between bez and trez tine in the case

of the red deer group, and at the thinnest point of the beam with other deer.

Girth taken just above the brow tine is most misleading. A horn is often very thick at that point and falls away miserably a little higher up.

Tip to Tip.—From tip to tip of highest point on each horn.

Widest inside or span.—From inside edge to inside edge at the widest point.

Spread.—Tip to tip of widest tines, or outside edge to outside edge at widest point.

Hollow horns :

Length.—The length of all hollow-horned Indian game animals is measured over the curve ; except blackbuck, which are measured straight from base to tip. All other length measurements are taken following the front curve of the horns from base to tip. With markhor follow the rib which starts at the back of the base.

With knobbed or ringed horns the tape is carried straight over the projections, and not pressed down between them—*e.g.* ibex and chinkara.

Girth.—Taken round the base of the horns.

Tip to tip.—Explains itself.

Spread or widest outside.—With the ox tribe this is taken from outer edge to outer edge at the widest point, the best way being to lay the head face down on a table and place a visiting card vertically at the point of measurement, marking the spot on the table. Then measure on the table the distance between the two spots.

Span.—Inside edge to inside edge at widest point.

Sweep.—Sometimes taken with bison. It is the measurement from tip to tip taken along the curves and across the forehead.

SKINNING THE HEAD.—Should be done as soon as possible, particularly in hot weather.

1. Cut the head-skin from the body-skin round the base of the neck.

2. Turn back the skin of the neck, then skin steadily and evenly all round the neck towards the head ; gradually pulling

the neck-skin back over the head towards the nose until the back of the head appears. Cut through the flesh all round the back of the head and throat, and then sever the head from the neck by dividing the spinal column from the base of the skull. Once the joint is visible a hard twist will often bring the head off.

So far the work has been done at the spot where the animal was shot, but now the whole head can be taken back to camp, and the skinning completed there. Carry on as follows:

Cut straight down the centre line of the back of the head from a point a little in front of the ears to the level of the angle of the jaw-bones. This cut should be made slightly to one side of a crest or the centre of a mane, if existent. It may also be taken right to the base of the neck-skin when the mask only is wanted; but as it should be kept as small as possible when the whole skin is to be kept, it is a good example to one's thick-headed followers to do the same with a mask, and may prevent them ruining a skin later on.

Then cut from the middle of the back of each horn to join the forward end of the centre cut.

If the bases of the horns are wide apart (as in deer), the first cut may start centrally between and level with them; but if they are close together, it is better to cut as above, and so leave a flap of skin at the back by which to hold and assist in skinning out, and for the taxidermist to sew on to when mounting the head.

Skin back from the cuts, turning back the hair from the base of the horns and separating the skin there by a jabbing motion of the point of the knife. Not a hair should be left behind.

Ears.—The ears are first obstacle met with. Skin these right up towards the tips as far as possible. When this is done the cartilage nearest the skin will appear white and quite free of flesh. Then cut back the muscles of the ear to its base and sever the cartilage at its base from the head. Leave the cartilage turned inside out.

Eyes.—Next skin forward until the inner white membrane of the eye-socket is reached. Pull this right out and cut it through as close as possible to the bone, taking great care not to damage the thin skin at the corners. Any fleshy thicknesses round the eyes must be fined down later when finishing up.

Eye-glands.—Then skin forward from the horns down the forehead until level with the forward edge of the eye-sockets. Here, if the head is that of a deer, antelope or sheep, there will be found an eye-gland on each side, which is often swollen and full of a greasy substance. Cut these clean out of their sockets close to the bone, and they will appear as lumps on the inside of the skin. If very oily it is better to shave them down right away, or they may exude grease all over the skin.

Muzzle.—Next come the corners of the mouth. Cut these away so that plenty of the inside of the lips is left with the skin. If the lips are cut away close to the margin of the hair, enough " turn-in " will not be left for the taxidermist to reproduce their natural shape ; so cut away close to the gum all round.

While skinning forward like this the nose will appear. Skin well forward and then cut through the nasal cartilage half an inch distant from the skin, then separate the whole skin from the head by cutting away the remaining portion of the lips close to the gums.

Finishing.—There is now left the nose and lips to skin out ; also, probably, a little flesh round the eyes.

To finish the nose. Sever the cartilage longitudinally between the nostrils and clean all flesh from between and around them, leaving them separated out and attached to the skin.

Then pare away all flesh and muscle from the lips, leaving the inner skin. Wherever the lips feel too thick between finger and thumb, divide them and shave away more flesh and tissue. Old safety-razor blades are the best instruments for all these finishing jobs.

Preserving.—The skin having now been thinned down so that the preservative can get into it, it must first be washed free of all blood. This may involve washing both sides of the skin, but it is absolutely necessary. Squeeze and press out as much water as possible, and, turning the skin, ears, nose and lips inside out, apply arsenical soap made into a thick cream to the lips, ears, muzzle and eyes ; rub burnt and powdered alum into the remainder of the skin. If a small skin use arsenical soap for all of it.

All preservative must be rubbed in thoroughly, the arsenical soap with a stiff brush.

With a very big skin such as a bison, it will be necessary to pare it down and score it deeply so as to allow the preservative to enter, and this may have to be done for several days running.

Next, stuff the mask (keeping it inside out) with dry grass or paper so that it is naturally distended (not stretched), and hang it up in the shade by a string passed through the nostrils, from a branch or tent pole. As soon as it has dried sufficiently to keep open, remove the grass or paper to allow a free air-passage. Change the stuffing daily if at all damp inside.

Burnt alum may be used for the whole of the mask, but the very thin parts are liable to crack. A skin can be saved with arsenical soap in any weather, whereas alum may fail in wet weather.

Preparing an entire Skin for Mounting or as a Flat Skin

1. Sketches and photographs. These are here invaluable. Animals should be carefully posed, not showing all leg and under parts to the camera.

2. Colouring of soft parts. Should be noted as in skinning a mask.

3. Body measurements. The first thing to do after shooting your animal is to measure it.

Measurements are essential to the taxidermist, as well as being of great scientific value.

Body measurements are taken as follows :

Lay the animal on its side, and on the flattest ground available. Pull it out straight without undue stretching, then release so as to relax naturally.

(a) *Length.*—Drive a peg into the ground at the end of the nose, a second at the base of the tail (where it bends up from the body), and a third at the tip of the tail, hair excluded. Measure the straight distance between the pegs, giving length of body and tail, and total length straight.

(*b*) Measure the length of the body along curves.

(*c*) *Height at shoulder.*—Place both fore heels together in as natural a standing position as possible. Drive in a peg at the top of the shoulder and another at the heels. Measure the straight distance between the pegs.

(*d*) *Girths.*—Throat.
Base of neck.
Chest.
Waist. (This is unreliable if there is much food in the stomach.)
Thigh (close to body).
Hock.
Cannon bone (at centre).
Shoulder (close to body).

(*e*) Hock to heel.

(*f*) Weigh also if possible.

SKINNING.—Skin as soon as possible.

Clean off as much blood as possible, and plug bullet-holes with grass or paper.

Lay the carcase on a bed of grass or cut boughs.

Cut through the skin from base of throat along centre of chest and centre line of belly to one side of testes, through the vent, and along underside of tail to its tip. This is the main median cut.

Cut from heel of each hoof or paw to just below elbow and hock respectively, then down the centres of inner sides of shoulders and thighs to join the main median cut.

Skin out the hind legs and tail first, and then forward.

Leave no flesh, and do not make holes in the skin.

Push away the skin from the body with the hand where possible, otherwise using the knife to sever the thin, semi-transparent tissue as it is pulled taut between the skin and the carcase.

Hoofs.—Skin the hoofs down to the last joint, and then sever from the leg-bones by thrusting the point of the knife into the joint and cutting through the tendons.

Skin the forelegs towards the body, still pulling the skin forward towards the head.

The whole body-skin ought now to be skinned away as far as the base of the neck. The remaining procedure is exactly as in taking off a mask, except that of course the mask is never severed from the body-skin, the whole skin being pulled forward over the neck to the base of the skull, and the head taken out through the cut at the back as before.

If the subject is not a horned animal, there is no necessity to make a cut at the back of the head, as the skin can be pulled straight over the skull.

If a flat skin only is wanted, the main median cut is carried along the throat and through the lower lip, so that the head is skinned out through that, the skull afterwards being cut away from the neck and cleaned.

Pads.—The feet have still to be skinned out.

If they are pads (as in carnivora) they must be skinned out to the end of the toes.

If for a flat skin, cut longitudinally through the centre of each pad, and skin right back to the toes, cutting away all flesh and tissue.

If the skin is to be mounted for museum purposes, cut along the junction of the large central pad and the hair on the inner side of the foot; then skin out the foot through this cut, leaving all bone below the wrist attached to the skin, but cutting away all flesh and tissue from between the joints and claws.

Hoofs.—Hoofs must be skinned out right to the end of the toes in both cases, and the bones taken out.

Leg-bones.—If the specimen is for a museum the leg-bones, both fore and hind, should be kept. All meat should be cleaned off them, they should be coated with preservative, tied in a bundle, labelled and hung up to dry.

Preserving the Skin.—If a flat skin is to be cured, it must be pegged out. First wash away all blood on both sides of the skin. Do this thoroughly.

Squeeze or press out all water, and, if necessary, dry the hair side in the sun for a little before pegging out, but be careful that the under side does not dry before pegging out, or before the preservative is applied. Preservative will not enter a dry skin.

Sew up all bullet-holes and rents.

Peg out the skin with 6-inch wire nails, pulling it out tight but not stretching it excessively.

Put the principal nails in in order; nose and root of tail, base of neck, tip of tail, sides, wrists.

When pegging out select the dryest place you can find, and, where possible, put straw or dry grass under the skin, but never any green or wet stuff.

The skin should not be pegged out in a hot sun, as that will make it dry too quickly without the preservative getting into it; or the fat in the skin may melt and soak down into it, then the hair will slip. Use may be made of the early morning sun in damp climates, stretching a blanket to shade the skin when the sun gets too hot. At great elevations (*e.g.* the Tibetan plateau) skins must often be dried in the sun, as if the skin be kept in the shade it may simply freeze.

In damp climates it is usually better to stretch the skin on a frame of four poles, usually bamboo. The skin is attached to the frame by strong string passed through small holes made along its edge. Long slips of green bamboo may be substituted for twine. Dry the skin between two small fires about 15 feet apart, the frame being stood up on edge between them.

Skins dried in this way need very careful watching. They may, being dried in a vertical position, fail to absorb the preservative, and consequently go wrong later if not put in pickle by the taxidermist as soon as received. Warning should be given accordingly.

Skins intended for mounting whole should not be pegged out, but hung on a frame to dry, the mask being filled with dry grass or paper. Two parallel, horizontal poles raised 3 feet off the ground, and a couple of feet apart, make a good frame for drying skins.

Having pegged out, stretched or otherwise spread the skin, apply preservative, rubbing it well in, and working it into every interstice between skin and bone in the feet, and later into any crack or fold which does not dry equally with the rest of the skin.

Preservative.—Several considerations influence the selection of a preservative. Climate, expense, the amount of transport

A bamboo shooting-hut. Upper Burma.

Tiger skins drying on bamboo frames.

To face page 88.

available, and whether the preservative can be purchased locally or not, are the principal ones.

Various preparations can be bought, such as Atlas mixture and Taxidermine, which are very good in any climate, but which involve extra transport, which is not always obtainable. They are also difficult to obtain outside a big city.

In a dry climate burnt alum is the best all-round article. It is obtainable almost anywhere, is easily prepared and easily carried. Supplement it with a little arsenical soap, and skins may be properly saved in any climate that is not extremely wet.

Arsenical soap by itself is a very good thing, but it has to be allowed for at the rate of a pound for an average skin, or two pounds for a large one. If masks only are to be collected, it is invaluable, and need only be carried at the rate of about three masks to the pound of arsenical soap.

Salt is not a good preservative. If the skin has to be kept for any length of time after being treated with salt, and the weather turn wet, then it will take up moisture from the air and go wrong. A skin treated with burnt alum and arsenical soap, or either alone, will stand any weather once it has been properly dried.

In very wet weather, salt, in the form of brine, is sometimes the only preservative which will save the skin. If cart transport and a large cask are available, then a very large skin, such as a bison, can be saved, or several small ones may be dealt with together. A cask is very hard to load and unload, and liable to upset on bad roads. Kerosene oil tins are much better. They are usually obtainable, easily carried, and will take any ordinary mask, while a whole tiger skin fits nicely into one, with a saturated solution of brine, and can be soldered up and despatched to the taxidermist in that form. One tin is, however, one cooli load, and, where transport is scarce, this is prohibitive.

If using brine, work the skin up and down in the tin or barrel so as to make it take up the brine, and change the brine every three or four days.

A substitute, which is really only a detergent and not a preservative, is wood ashes. This is almost always available, and in considerable quantities. Ashes from resinous woods should not be used. Any others should be worked into the skin until it will take up no more. For removing the fat from a Himalayan bear ashes are invaluable. A skin may take three or four days' rubbing with ashes and flat stones to extract the fat, but it is worth it, and it is the only method with a fat bear shot in late autumn.

Recipes.—Burnt alum. To prepare alum for rubbing into a skin, break it up into small pieces and roast a little at a time (on an iron plate) over a fire. It will bubble up. Continue roasting until it ceases to bubble and is quite hard again, then take it off and pound it into a fine powder. Ten pounds of alum makes about seven pounds of burnt alum.

Brine. Dissolve equal quantities of salt and alum, at the rate of one pound of each to the gallon, bring to the boil and cool.

Skulls.—It is not advisable to bleach or macerate skulls in the field. It leads to loss of teeth.

Cut off all the removable flesh. Take out the brain through the orifice at the back by pushing a stick into it and stirring them up, then shaking out the resultant porridge. Pouring hot water into the brain-case and shaking it out again will help greatly to bring away the contents. Do not give this job to an ignorant native to do, unless he has done it before correctly in your presence. If he has not, he will inevitably chop off the back of the skull with an axe in order to get at the brains.

Wash the skull and hang up to dry, after tying the lower jaw-bone firmly on to it. It may be a good plan to coat it with preservative.

TEETH.—The canine teeth of carnivora, and the tushes of boar soon split and fall to pieces unless prevented from drying too rapidly.

Wrap them round with waxed tape or strips of linen, or coat them over with melted wax.

ELEPHANTS' FEET.—The feet of elephants may be turned into useful trophies, such as stools or waste-paper baskets.

To skin an elephant's foot, sever the skin round the foot about 15 inches from the ground. Cut all the way down the back of the foot, and skin out as with other animals. Be careful to remove all flesh right down to the point of the toes. It may be necessary to divide the sole or cut it away from one side of the foot.

Coat both sides of the skin with preservative and dry in the shade. If there is dry sand or ashes handy, fill up the foot to the original shape before drying.

The same remarks apply to the feet of rhinoceros.

Packing a Skin.—Never pack skins and skulls together.

Fold the legs over the centre and roll up the skin from the tail, leaving the mask outside. Tie round with cord and place in a sack.

If a big skin, it may only fold across the centre and be impossible to roll.

Always remember to give skins an airing at least once every ten days. Place in the sun, hair uppermost.

When loading a skin on to pack transport, it must be remembered that it is very brittle if properly dry. If undue pressure is brought to bear on such parts as the eyes or corners of the mouth, they will split.

Care of Trophies.—All heads and skins which are hung on a wall need looking after, or they will be ruined by insects.

They should be brushed frequently, to remove dust. Every three months turpentine or, if not available, kerosene oil, must be rubbed well into the hair with the finger-tips.

Where hollow horns are removable, turpentine or kerosene oil should be poured from one to the other every six months, and a plug soaked in one of them left in the horn.

If not removable, inspect them and wipe over with a strong solution of corrosive sublimate or with turpentine. A strong solution of corrosive sublimate must be squirted into any crevices, and particularly into any little round holes which appear. These are the homes of destructive insects.

This may be a little troublesome, but good trophies are worth the trouble.

To Macerate a Skull.—This is done by leaving the skull in water until the remaining flesh decays. The water should be changed every few days until all the flesh has disappeared.

If the skull turns black, the colour will disappear if put into the sun to dry.

To bleach, leave in the sun and water two or three times a day. This is a long process, and it is shorter to dip the skull in boiling water containing a double handful of washing soda. Then start a small fire and, sprinkling a little flowers of sulphur on it, hold the skull in the smoke for ten minutes, then put in the sun.

TONGUES.—In the case of carnivora it is useful to keep the tongue if the specimen is to be mounted with the mouth open.

Take out the tongue from the skull after skinning the head and skin, and dry it just like any other skin.

Better still, if spirit is available, cut away superfluous meat and preserve in spirit.

In the case of drying the skin of the tongue, coat it with preservative.

PART II

PREFACE

The following accounts of individual species are necessarily curtailed for reasons of space.

They are not intended to be zoological treatises, but to give the beginner a good idea of the appearance, size and habits of the animal, and where he is likely to find it.

References to other works have had to be almost entirely omitted, again for want of space.

Of the fifty-four species dealt with, the author has shot thirty-six, and has personal acquaintance with eight more; the accounts of the remainder have been compiled from the personal narratives or the writings of others.

THE INDIAN ELEPHANT

(*Elephas maximus*)

VERNACULAR NAMES.—*Hathi*, Hindostani ; *Ane*, Tamil ; *Hsin*, Burmese.

DESCRIPTION.—It is unnecessary to give a detailed description of the elephant, but some points of interest may be noted.

The scientific name *maximus* is not really applicable, as the African elephant is the bigger species of the two. The largest Indian elephant known was the Bulrampore fighting elephant, whose skeleton is now in the Calcutta Museum, and is 12 feet in height. One of 11 feet is recorded from Gahrwal, and one of 10 feet 8 inches was shot by Major Evans in Upper Burma. The average height of a fully grown male can, however, be taken to be about 9 feet 4 inches.

There are several old tusks of over 8 feet on record, and one of 7 feet 3½ inches weighing 102 lb. The best pair of recent years were found in Coimbatore, with the bones of the bull which had owned them, and appeared to have been there a year, so had lost a good deal of weight by drying. They were a beautifully symmetrical pair, measuring—right, 7 feet 8 inches ; left, 7 feet 10 inches ; and weighing 79½ lb. and 82½ lb. respectively.

Cows stand about 8 feet as a rule.

DISTRIBUTION.—Elephants have almost disappeared from the Central Provinces, while a few herds still exist in Behar and Orissa. On the west they do not go north of Canara, but have increased there of recent years. Further south, in Coimbatore, Mysore, the Nilgiris and Travancore, they are plentiful, and usually an unmitigated nuisance. In the Northern Circars there are still some herds.

On the N.E. elephants are to be found from the Dun, along the base of the hills through Assam and Burma, to Malaya.

Habits and Characteristics.—I regret I cannot share the usual high opinion of the elephant. To me elephants are unpleasant nuisances, with entire want of that nobility which seems to have been ascribed to them solely through their bulk.

They are moderately intelligent, highly temperamental, subject to fits of unreasoning rage or panic. They are intensely destructive to cultivation and forests, and, if it had not been for their usefulness in extracting timber for commercial profit, they would by now be restricted to the most remote jungles.

In places, such as bison ground at the foot of the Nilgiris or when hunting in Upper Burma, I have found them a perfect curse; being chivied out of good ground by irate cows, or held up by a herd pulling down bamboos all over the line of the animal I was tracking. I was nearly run over by a herd of twenty-one in N. Canara in 1923 when walking peacefully back to camp.

Shooting elephant has never appealed to me, though it has a great fascination for many men, and undoubtedly has its thrill and interest.

I can only repeat what I have been told by others, and learnt by studying the skulls of shot animals. The elephant's brain is the mark to try for. It is about the size and shape of a Rugby football, and situated low down in the back of the head. The two easy lines to it are via the nostrils or the ear orifice.

To reach the brain via the nostrils, a frontal shot must be taken. If level with the head, aim at the saucer-like depression between the eyes. If below, fire through the boss at the base of the trunk.

The ear shot should be taken broadside on. If exactly broadside on, then directly, but allowance being made for standing out of direct line.

The heart shot is used effectively by many, but needs accurate anatomical knowledge, as the heart is situated lower and further forward than might be expected, and is also small for the size of the beast.

Any one intending to take up elephant shooting should study Evans' *Big Game Shooting in Upper Burma*.

As an aid to big game shooting, when domesticated, either

for beating or for transport, the elephant is famous, and in many places indispensable. It is almost impossible to tackle animals in high grass without elephants, but, as a rule, the expense of hiring and feeding is quite beyond the pocket of the average sportsman in India. Consequently, one is dependent on the kind offices of Government officials or Indian chiefs for this class of shooting, and it can hardly be said to enter into the scope of this book. Much less does the "ringing" of tigers by a large number of elephants, such as is done in Nepal, as many as 450 being employed.

As a transport animal in thick forest and hills the elephant is invaluable. In the wild state they ascend to 10,000 feet at times, and their sure-footedness on a hill-side is wonderful, while their strength enables them to remove obstacles with ease, and their "clearance" takes them over a fallen trunk or boulder which is impassable to a pony or mule. They are also practically immune from the attacks of tigers, when adult.

I would, however, advise any one who is travelling with elephants to be careful about approaching them if the mahout is not with them. They are often uncertain tempered, particularly in South Burma, and I have twice had to travel with a beast that was quite unapproachable when grazing except by his driver, and when coming back to camp the greatest care had to be taken not to bump into him. Such beasts are a great nuisance, as even their drivers cannot take them up in the dark when grazing; consequently, a late start is inevitable, and a short march if the weather is hot.

Just to show the temperamental nature of elephants, the following may be of interest.

While travelling in Western Siam in February 1924, with five baggage elephants, I camped on the banks of a river. The elephants were off-loaded and turned out to graze in a big patch of grass and sand, while I set off down stream to fish. About ten minutes later I was startled by a chorus of trumpeting and screaming, and ran back thinking something dreadful was happening. I found my five elephants in a semi-circle creating a terrible din, with the cause of the uproar crawling on the sand in front of them. It was a tortoise about a foot long!

A few days later the same elephants faced a tiger with

absolute equanimity, while three weeks later a herd of bison, bolting some fifty yards from the track, stampeded them so far into the forest that it took me two days to recover my discarded baggage.

Useful facts to remember when elephant shooting are that they have very poor eyesight, fair hearing, and excellent scenting powers.

Twice the circumference of the forefoot gives the height of an elephant.

A shootable elephant will have 18 inches of tusk showing and 2 feet not visible; the tusk should weigh about 40 lb.

If a herd stampedes in your direction keep still. To run is fatal. A shot into the base of the trunk will turn a charging elephant.

If you have to run, go downhill; an elephant cannot travel fast or control his course well on a down grade.

Elephant shooting is not allowed in any district where "kheddars" are held, but may be shot in parts of Burma under special licence, and there are always a good many declared rogues in Coimbatore and other adjacent districts.

THE GREAT INDIAN RHINOCEROS
(*Rhinoceros unicornis*)

THE JAVAN RHINOCEROS
(*Rhinoceros sondaicus*)

THE SUMATRAN RHINOCEROS
(*Rhinoceros sumatrensis*)

Vernacular Names.—*Gainda*, Hindostani; *Kyan*, Burmese.

Description.—The general appearance of a rhinoceros is well known, so it is only necessary to note the differences between the three species.

R. unicornis is the largest of the three species, running to 6½ feet at the shoulders, while *R. sondaicus* does not measure more than 6 feet, and *R. sumatrensis*, which has two horns, to the single one of each of the other species, stands only about 4½ feet.

R. unicornis has a skin folded so as to resemble armour-plating, and it is also covered with little studs.

R. sondaicus has the folds but not the studs, the skin being netted all over with fine cracks.

The skin of *R. sumatrensis* is blacker, rather hairy, and in texture more like the surface of an orange.

The horn of *R. unicornis* runs to 25 inches in length and 21 inches basal circumference, but 16 inches is a good horn, and few go bigger than this.

R. sondaicus has a more slender horn, which reaches nearly 11 inches in length.

R. sumatrensis has two horns, of which the longer front one usually attains a length of about 14 inches. There are two much longer horns in the British Museum which are ascribed to this species, but they were purchased in Malaya, and appear to me to be typical horns of the African Black Rhinoceros from the lower slopes of Kenia.

Asiatic rhinoceros horns are of considerable value for medicinal purposes in Eastern Asia, and African horns are imported and sold as Asiatic horns. The longer horns are, however, almost invariably rejected as not genuine. I have seen a good many authentic horns of *R. sumatrensis*, and met sportsmen who have shot them, and have never seen or heard of one of more than 14½ inches.

Distribution.—*R. unicornis* is still plentiful in the Nepal Terai, and is found along the foot of the Himalayas to Assam, where it was once plentiful, but has been so reduced in numbers that the shooting has been closed. It does not appear to reach Burma.

R. sondaicus is found from the Sikkim Terai and the Sunderbunds throughout Assam and Burma to Malaya.

R. sumatrensis is found from Chittagong and Eastern Assam throughout Burma to Malaya.

Habits and Characteristics.—*R. unicornis* is essentially a dweller in high grass, in which it makes tunnels like enormous rabbit-holes. They have a trick of depositing their ordure at one place, piles several feet high being found. Many have been shot by men waiting at these. They are usually driven by elephants, and numbers have been shot by "ringing" in the Nepal Terai.

They are usually peaceful beasts, but will sometimes charge an elephant and rip it badly with their lower tusks.

R. sondaicus has a great range, and is found in swamp or on ridges 5000 feet above sea-level. Forest and somewhere to wallow are what they need.

R. sumatrensis seems to stick to the hills.

Both these species are shy and retiring, but will charge freely when wounded.

They have been terribly poached of late years, and the shooting of them is now forbidden in Burma. The only permit I know of being granted of recent years was to a monied American who shot a cow with a small calf, which, of course, also died. In lower Burma and the Malay Peninsula, they are much caught in pits, and by poachers sitting up over salt-licks. Every part is saleable for medicinal purposes, the blood and horns being particularly valuable.

Their period of gestation is reported to be fifteen months for *R. unicornis*, and seven and a half months for *R. sumatrensis*. The period seems to be very small for the last species. I do not know on what evidence these are based.

Only one calf is produced at a birth.

All species are very easily killed. A chest shot, breaking up the big blood-vessels, is quickly fatal.

THE MALAY TAPIR

(*Tapirus indicus*)

VERNACULAR NAME.—*Tara kyan*, Burmese.

DESCRIPTION.—A parti-coloured, pig-like beast about 40 inches at the shoulder, with a prolonged nose, which almost amounts to a trunk. The fore-part to the shoulders is black, behind the shoulders it is greyish white, except for the lower half of the hind limbs. The hair is very scanty, the impression being given that the body is naked.

DISTRIBUTION.—In the Indian Empire it is found in Mergui and Southern Tenasserim. It is also found in Western Siam, the Malay Peninsula and Sumatra.

HABITS AND CHARACTERISTICS.—I have frequently come across the tracks of this animal in Tenasserim and Siam. It appears to stick to valleys and dense evergreen jungle as a rule. I had a glimpse of one in Tenasserim, and later saw one which had been shot by an American sitting up at night over a salt-lick. A few days later I was on the march about fifteen miles further north, and had only left camp about half an hour before, when my terrier dashed into the evergreen and began barking furiously about twenty yards away. I went towards him and made out a patch of white a few feet beyond him, and then suddenly discovered the fore-half of a tapir within ten yards of me. It had its head down and was gazing stupidly at the dog, which was barking within a couple of feet of its nose. If I had shot it, I should have had to camp for two days at least, to skin and preserve the entire specimen; so as I had a servant with me seriously ill with dysentery, whom it was imperative to get down to habitations as soon as possible, I stood and watched the strange animal for about a minute and a half, before it lumbered off into the forest. I had previously found many tracks of this or another of these animals close to my camp, and, on following them up, they invariably led into the densest evergreen jungle. I should say that they owe their continued existence much more to their living in thick cover than to any alertness.

THE KIANG OR TIBETAN WILD ASS

(*Equus kiang*)

VERNACULAR NAME.—*Kiang*, Ladakhi and Tibetan.

DESCRIPTION.—Height about 13 hands, with a large, ugly fiddle-head; a long coarse tail and dark mane. General colour reddish sandy. Muzzle and under parts, white.

DISTRIBUTION.—The Tibetan plateau; above 12,000 feet. Plentiful in the Rupshu district of Ladakh.

HABITS AND CHARACTERISTICS.—These are all unpleasant where they concern the sportsman, and a description of the beast is inserted, not because it is in any way a game animal, but to enable those who have a stalk spoilt by these irritating, inquisitive brutes, to know what they are swearing at.

No sooner does one of these ugly brutes see a sportsman taking cover to stalk an *Ovis ammon* or goa, not only does he come and prance round him, but fetches all his pals to play at circus, with the result of sending off the object of the stalk.

They are very hardy, but have shown such vicious disposition in captivity as to be useless for domestication.

THE INDIAN WILD ASS

(*Equus onager indicus*)

VERNACULAR NAMES.—*Jangli gadha*, Hindostani ; *Ghorkhar*, Sind and Baluchistan.

DESCRIPTION.—Standing about 11 hands, this is a much handsomer beast than the last. The back and neck are sandy, shading into white on the buttocks and under parts. A broad dark dorsal stripe.

DISTRIBUTION.—The deserts of N.W. Rajputana and Sind, and Cutch. Westwards, more scantily, to Baluchistan.

HABITS AND CHARACTERISTICS.—This desert-dwelling animal is seldom seen by the average sportsman, and a description is only inserted as it may turn up when *en route* to shooting-grounds near its habitat.

THE GAUR OR INDIAN BISON

(*Bos gaurus*)

VERNACULAR NAMES.—*Gaur*, Hindostani ; *Ban boda*, Central India ; *Kathu*, Malabar ; *Kulga*, Canara and Western Ghats ; *Pyoung*, Burmese ; *Mitnan*, Assam.

DESCRIPTION.—The bulls of this grand species reach 19 hands in height in India, while over 20 hands has been recorded from Assam and Burma. The maximum with cows appears to be 17 hands.

They are heavily built, short-legged animals, with a high dorsal ridge, which amounts to a hump in the bulls. The general colour is black for bulls and dark brown for cows, while the calves are bright chestnut. Both sexes have white stockings. The forehead and crown are ashy or yellowish grey.

Many old bulls have a dewlap, but it is an individual characteristic, and in no way a distinctive racial feature. A few bulls have spots about the neck, while one or two turn up with a tuft of hair on the throat.

The iris of the eye is brown, but, owing to a certain density and clouding of the cornea, the eye appears bluish in some lights.

The horns rise wide apart and curve up and inward at the points, though I have seen two heads of which the horns were almost at right angles to the face throughout their length. One of these came from Assam, and the other from Siam. The maximum dimensions of the horns are about 40 inches length, 20 inches girth, and 50 inches spread; but such dimensions have never been recorded in any one head, and a trophy which measures 30 inches in length, 18 inches girth, and 39 inches across can be considered as much above the average. The length is not a great factor in assessing a trophy, as horns of old bulls are often much worn down at the ends, and spread is usually taken as the chief desideratum in a head.

The horns are much corrugated at the base only, being smooth for three-quarters of their length, and are black at base and tip, grading into golden yellow or olive green at the middle. They are very handsome when well polished.

Distribution.—Throughout the hilly districts of Burma and Malaya. In India they are found in suitable country from Khandesh on the west and Northern Bengal on the east, southwards through the Peninsula. They are still plentiful in parts of Assam, from which province, with Burma and Coimbatore, the best heads usually come.

Habits and Characteristics.—The gaur is a shy beast, avoiding the habitations of man as a rule, though this does not always apply, as, in S. India, they may be seen, from more than one planter's bungalow verandah, grazing on the hill-side in the Anamalais or Coorg.

There is one thing necessary to them, and that is a combination of hills and forest.

The cows and young bulls live in herds of four or five up to about fifteen as a rule; the old bulls, as with tsine, living solitary for the greater part of the year, but periodically rejoining a herd in search of a cow. They may then find a younger bull approaching maturity, and drive him from the herd after a fight. The young bull may then be found living alone, so that it is not quite safe to assume that every solitary bull is an old one.

The period of gestation is probably about eleven months.

Bulls also go about in pairs at times, and they may both be large, or one small and one large. The former is the more probable.

I once tracked up two bulls in N. Canara, and had got up within 150 yards in fairly thick jungle, when a terrific series of screaming bellows broke out from their direction and was immediately answered from what were evidently two more bulls about thirty yards from them. The noise was very like elephants trumpeting, and the two Canarese with me promptly yelled " Hathi, hathi ", and fled. The bulls were making such a noise that I do not think they would have heard them, but the men ran right across the wind, and, although I dashed in as quick as I could, I was only in time to see, by jumping on a fallen tree, the heads of four fine bulls as they crashed off in line abreast through the young cane.

I have only once again heard this noise, and it was from a solitary bull in the Tenasserim hill in January 1924. I think there is little doubt that it is a challenging note.

The bull also grunts loudly when feeding in cover, while he is very noisy, breaking sticks and trampling undergrowth. Yet a dry twig snapping under the hunter's foot will frighten him, and he will slip quietly away.

Bison are also reported to make a piping, whistling noise when feeding, but I have not heard this myself. It is recorded by Dunbar Brander and other reliable observers.

If a bison is frightened and bolts just as you are getting up to him, run in hard. He will almost invariably pull up for a look round after going seventy or eighty yards.

Bison form an excellent test for the tracker, as they do not feed very fast, and have a big and well-defined track. They are also very wary, though they are not nearly as difficult to approach as tsine.

Ordinarily they are timid, inoffensive beasts, but a wounded bull will charge savagely and, on occasions, hunt a man persistently. They also have the usual trick of all wild oxen, whereby they go back on their tracks and ambush the hunter from a patch of thick cover as he passes. I have known of three Europeans who were killed by this trick.

Look for him where a combination of good food and freedom from flies is to be obtained, in jungle-covered hills.

Leeches will drive them on to the open slopes or into bamboo forest. Young bamboo shoots are much favoured as a diet in the middle of the rains, while the new growth of grass on a burnt hill-side is an unfailing attraction. Above all they like quiet, and in most places it is essential to camp well away from villages to find a good bull within reach of a day's shooting.

They have excellent noses, fine hearing, and poor eyesight.

The greatest care should be taken to avoid shooting cows instead of bulls. The only safe guide is the horns, and even when following a solitary bull it is not safe to fire until they are seen, as the following will show.

I was wanting a specimen of a bull gaur for mounting in the Prince of Wales Museum in Bombay, and was after serow on the Tenasserim-Siam border, when I came on fresh tracks of a solitary bull. Following these up along the crest of a ridge, they eventually turned down into a wide hollow full of bamboo and high undergrowth. Entering this, I had gone about 100 yards down the slope when I put up a couple of jungle fowl, which flew off with a great clatter. I halted immediately, and made out the face of a gaur, framod in an opening in the bamboos, looking at me from about seventy yards away. I could not see the horns, but as far as I knew there was no other animal but a bull in question, so sighted under the chin and fired. To my surprise, two bison made off. Following up a heavy blood-trail, I came on my beast 400 yards on, thrashing about in a clump of young cane on top of a ridge, and went in and finished it. I then found to my disgust, that I had shot a very big cow, with 23½-inch horns, 26 inches across. This would not have happened if I had been shooting for a trophy, as it was only the skin I wanted for mounting; but it shows the result of the want of a little care.

Incidentally, the skull was taken out of my camp by a tiger on a very dark and rainy night a fortnight later. What the attraction was, beyond a peculiarly unpleasant smell, it is hard to understand, as all the meat had been cut and scraped off it.

There are still a good many gaur left, but it is a pity to shoot more than a few specimens of such a fine animal; so, after defeating one or two by one's own unaided efforts, pass on to some other species.

TSINE OR BANTING

(*Bos sondaicus*)

VERNACULAR NAME.—*Tsaing*, Burmese.

DESCRIPTION.—Tsine resemble a large and "gamey" breed of domestic cattle, and are, in all probability, the ancestors of domesticated breeds of Asia.

The tsine has no hump or pronounced dorsal ridge, and little or no dewlap.

The bull stands up to 17 hands at the shoulder, and the cow about six inches less.

Cows are usually foxy red, but occasionally much darker individuals are seen which are almost liver-coloured.

Bulls vary very greatly. When young they are of the same colour as the cows; and, while in some the colour gets lighter with age, so that they become khaki for life, others turn French grey and then darken to "buffalo" blue, while a proportion darken to a copper-beech shade without any intermediate phase and, continuing the process, become chocolate brown. In all except the khaki-coloured bulls, there is an obvious tendency towards melanism, and black bulls occasionally turn up in Burma, while they are common in Malaya.

Both sexes have white stockings, and an oval white disc on the buttocks.

The horns of the cows are much like those of domestic cattle, the points turning inwards to such an extent that they are sometimes crossed.

The horns of the bull are wide-spread as a rule, with an upright curve. They vary in girth from 14 to 20 inches, and specimens of all types may be found in the same area. This is also the case with the different colour phases. A good head will be 25 inches in length, with a girth of over 15 and a spread of 36 inches.

There is a hard and naked callous patch of skin between the bases of the horns, which is very distinctive of this species.

HABITS AND CHARACTERISTICS.—Tsine live mainly in foot-hills and fairly open forest, though some of the old bulls retire periodically to the higher hills. They do not go as high as gaur as a rule, and are, unlike gaur, not very shy of human habitations.

The cows and young bulls are to be found in herds of about five to fifteen, though I have seen one herd of over thirty. The old bulls are usually solitary, but are also to be found two together. They periodically join a herd to find a cow in season, and then take her off for a few days into the forest.

Pairing takes place in the rains as a rule, but may occur at any time of the year.

The period of gestation is about ten months, and there is one calf normally, though I have once seen twins.

Bulls are pugnacious, and I once came on a tremendous fight between a grey and a chocolate-brown bull. The ground was very torn up, and clots of blood flung in every direction. I could find no traces of the presence of a cow, or any reason for the strife.

Tsine provide the finest sport of any beast I know, and I consider an old bull the most difficult animal to bag on foot (not from an elephant, that is not fair) of all the big game of the Indian Empire.

They are very wary, and can be very dangerous. They feed fast, lie down at unexpected times and at carefully selected places, and are altogether much more difficult to bring to book than any gaur. Add to this that the hunter has usually to do most or all of his own tracking, owing to the absence of efficient native help, and I think my contention will be admitted, that he provides the finest test of a hunter's ability.

Tsine are usually fairly plentiful where found, and the discovery of fresh tracks is moderately simple, but the old bull feeds fast and, consequently, a fast rate of tracking must be maintained with the risk of more noise.

The tops of ridges are favourite places for them to feed in the early rains, which is the ideal season for their pursuit, but in the latter half of July the young bamboos begin to sprout, and the tsine, particularly the old bulls, are then to be found in the wide bottoms of the nullahs, feeding greedily on the new shoots. They can then often be located by the twang of a breaking bamboo, and the open nature of the forest makes them easier to approach.

If they are frightened and bolt, it is always worth while running after them, as they will often pull up after going eighty yards or so; or, if they have fled from the top of a ridge, a shot into the broad back of the bull may be obtained as he climbs the opposite slope of the nullah beyond.

Tsine are rather noisy feeders as a rule, but can move with great quietness in thick forest.

I once came on a herd of about fifteen tsine in the early morning, and got to within twenty yards of them in some grass about two feet high. They all fed past me as I lay behind a small ant-hill, and, not being satisfied that the particular old bull I was after was with them, I crawled in among them again. They were feeding peacefully, and I had reached the cover of a fair-sized bush, when they suddenly became absolutely silent. All the breaking of twigs and munching ceased, and every beast was quite motionless. I particularly remember the heads of two young bulls silhouetted against a patch of light, with the ends of some bamboos held unbitten in their mouths, so that the branches were prevented from springing back. I had heard no warning sound from any of them, and, as I had not shifted position for several minutes, I have no idea what had alarmed them or how the warning had simultaneously been conveyed to the whole herd. They could not all have got my wind at the same time, as it was a still morning and they were spread out all round me. Suddenly there was a terrific snort from the other side of my bush which almost seemed to blow me off the ground, and away went an old cow, which had been feeding within a few feet of me, taking the herd with her. There was great crashing of boughs for about fifty yards and then all sound seemed to cease; although, as examination of their tracks showed, their pace had not decreased or the nature of the forest altered.

The charge of an old bull tsine can be dodged on favourable ground, but he may hunt one, and it is desirable to have a tree handy to put between you on these occasions.

I was once after bison in a remote part of the dry zone, and frequently crossed the tracks of an old bull tsine during the morning. He was solitary, and I had seen no other tsine tracks within several miles, which was curious.

As I could find no fresh gaur tracks, I took up some twenty-four-hour-old tracks of this tsine about midday, and followed them for about an hour to the flat top of a ridge, where I decided to sit down and have lunch. I had handed over the rifle to the Burman gun-bearer, and turned to call to the tiffin-cooli, who was about 100 yards down the slope of the ridge, when a noise behind me made me look over my shoulder, just as a fine khaki-coloured bull tsine burst out of a patch of young cane and came straight for me. The Burman tried to run and I had only time to grab the rifle from him, when the bull, who had only started from about thirty yards away, was on top of me. I jumped aside, expecting to be able to whip round and put one behind his ribs as he went on, but he turned like a polo pony, and I only just succeeded in dodging him. He then hunted me in and out of the bamboo clumps, forcing me to a display of agility which, I feel sure, would have won me unstinted applause in the Madrid bull-ring, and I only saved myself by diving sideways between two clumps of bamboo. He then treed all the Burmans, and, having picked myself up, I put a bullet into him, but too low and far back. He then went off, evidently very sick, and I followed him up, being full of wrath at his treatment of me. He had lain down twice in a little over a mile, and I felt sure of getting him, when a tremendous thunderstorm burst and washed out all the tracks, so that I had to give up the attempt.

This is the only unprovoked attack I have had made on me in twenty-five years' shooting, and I think it probable that this bull had been wounded by some native hunter, and had gone off by himself to get over it, with a naturally soured temper.

I strongly recommend a trip after tsine to any enthusiast who has had some experience, and wants to try out the knowledge he has acquired in the most fascinating way possible.

THE YAK

(*Bos grunniens*)

VERNACULAR NAME.—*Dong*, Ladakhi.

DESCRIPTION.—A big, lumpy black beast, with masses of hair almost sweeping the ground growing from shoulders, thighs, belly and tail, the bull stands about 16 hands, the cow about 14 hands. The head is held low and forward, while the horns curve forward and upward, turning well in at the points. The best head recorded is 40 inches in length, with a girth of 18 inches. I have seen a dozen or more ranging from 30 to 36 inches, with girths of 16½ to 18 inches.

DISTRIBUTION.—The wild yak now only enters the Indian Empire as an autumn migrant from Tibet, and seems to be limited to the Changchemmo valley in N.E. Ladakh and, very occasionally, the valleys east of the Karakoram Pass.

As they are sacred (being cattle) in Kashmir, they may not be shot there. They are still very numerous towards the Horpa Tso in Tibet, and further north in the Kuen Luen mountains, which are practically inaccessible in these days.

HABITS AND CHARACTERISTICS.—There is little known about the wild yak, and all I have been able to gather from the three or four sportsmen I have met who have shot them, is that they have wonderful powers of scent, acute hearing and poor eye-sight. They will charge when wounded, but are normally timid.

The yak has got the name of *Bos grunniens* or "grunting ox" from, I presume, the grunting of the tame animal; which also makes horrible teeth-grinding noises, and render them a nuisance near one's tent at night.

They are extremely useful as beasts of burden, but will not stand long marches. When tired they will simply lie down and decline to move, which is awkward when far from water.

THE NYAN OR TIBETAN WILD SHEEP

(*Ovis ammon hodgsoni*)

VERNACULAR NAME.—*Nyan*, Ladakhi.

DESCRIPTION.—This grand sheep stands as much as 46½ inches at the shoulder, this being the height of the one illustrated, which was shot on the Kyangchu Plain in Ladakh. It weighed 240 lb.; horns, 40½ inches.

The general colour is greyish brown in winter and reddish grey in summer. The thick winter coat is shed in quantities in July, and I have found masses of it lying where a band of rams had just been resting.

An old ram carries a white ruff, the depth of which varies very much with the season, and in mid-August it is often inconspicuous. There is a dark stripe along the spine, and the under parts are lighter to white.

The horns are very massive, and usually curve close up to the sides of the head; the points, in very large specimens, pass the eye, and must considerably impede the animal's vision. In judging a head, it is essential that the points turn up. In the specimen illustrated, it will be noticed that the point of the left horn, although broken, rises above the bridge of the nose, the right horn is more broken and the point is towards the camera, so is very hard to judge.

Unfortunately, most old rams have the points broken, as they are great fighters.

The best head I know of was a 52½, which was shot in Ladakh in 1920, and left by the owner in a skin merchant's shop in Srinagar for some years, until it was destroyed in a fire in 1924. A 51½ was killed in 1924 by a gunner officer.

The biggest recorded is a picked-up head measuring 57 inches, which heads the list in Ward's *Records of Big Game*, but I doubt this being a "hodgsoni" head; from the circumstances attending its collection, I think it was probably a head of a more northerly race, brought down and discarded by a trader.

Any head over 40 inches is a good one, and 38 inches can be considered shootable, but the massiveness of the head is a great consideration; a girth of 18 inches is good.

Ewes carry small horns up to a foot in length.

DISTRIBUTION.—*Ovis ammon hodgsoni* is found from a little east of the Karakoran Pass, right along the south side of the Tibetan plateau to the vicinity of Lhasa. They come into the northern portions of Zanshar, Lahoul and Spiti in the summer, and migrate to the Indus valley, Tsotso and Chumurti in the winter. Further south they may be found in the vicinity of Gyantse in the summer. They suffered very severely from foot-and-mouth disease in 1910, but have recovered, and are now as numerous as ever in the Indus valley from a point about fifty miles from Leh. They are locally migratory, and ground which holds good rams in the spring may hold nothing but ewes in the autumn. Old rams are usually in small bands up to six in number, and two old rams are often found living together.

The rut is in September and October, and the kids, usually only one, but sometimes two, are born in May.

Ovis ammon feed largely on grass, and follow good grazing; they have also a great liking for a small whitish thistle, which grows close to the ground, at between 15,000 and 17,000 feet.

They begin feeding very early in the day, before sunrise as a rule in summer, and lie down on some commanding ridge or hill-side from about ten to four, when they again begin to feed.

They are hard to make out, and great patience and care must be exercised. They have fine eyesight, and their scenting powers are their chief defence, being much assisted by the ever-changing winds blowing off the glaciers.

The country they inhabit is open, and if disturbed they travel a very long way. I once followed on the tracks of two I had disturbed for about twenty-five miles, taking my camp with me, and they had never stopped to feed.

It is no use marching many miles to ammon ground and then hurrying matters. Do not be discouraged if nothing is seen for two or three days. Work the ground slowly, particularly examining the cup-like hollows near the tops of the hills, which hold their favourite thistles. It is better to see nothing at all on your ground than ewes, in midsummer at all events, for they are hardly ever near the old rams.

Old rams are usually distinguishable by their white ruffs at a considerable distance, and also give themselves away by the clash of their horns when fighting. The sound of an encounter can be heard a mile away at times. I once watched a fight between two very fine rams with glasses from about 100 yards away, and was amazed at the force with which they charged each other and met head to head.

The horns of a good ram always look too big and heavy for

him, and they carry their heads with rather a droop when walking. The lowest I have known *Ovis ammon* to descend is 12,000 feet, and I have seen them at 19,000 feet.

They give grand sport and carry a fine trophy, while, although the climate is severe owing to the altitude and great changes of temperature, yet the ground they live on is of a nature which entails no climbing, only steady walking and endurance.

THE BUFFALO

(*Bos bubalis*)

Vernacular Names.—*Jangli bhainsa*, Hindostani; *Arna*, Central India; *Moh*, Assam; *Taw kyouay*, Burma.

Description.—A finely built, heavy, and altogether high-class edition of the common Indian water-buffalo, the wild animal stands 16 to 16½ hands at the shoulder, and weighs about 2000 lb.

The horns are of the same type as in the common water-buffalo, but are much thicker and finer. They are not laid back to the same extent, but are almost square with the head. The best horn on record measures 77⅝ inches in length, but may have been from one of the semi-wild herds (such as those belonging to the Todas in the Nilgiris), which occasionally attain great length. The best modern heads are two from Assam, measuring 140½ inches and 134 inches round the "sweep". The greatest girth recorded is 23 inches, and 20 inches is a good girth for a head, anything over 100 inches round the sweep being good.

Distribution.—The south-eastern portions of Central India, the Northern Circars, Orissa, N.E. Bengal, the Sunderbunds and Assam. There are a few in the lower Irawadi valley and delta, and also in W. Siam.

Habits and Characteristics.—I have never shot a wild buffalo, though I have hunted them unsuccessfully on two or three occasions in places where they were scarce and insufficient time available. They are almost entirely grass feeders, and usually stick to low ground in the vicinity of rivers. They have decreased very greatly of late years in Central India through disease and shooting, but may now be said to be once again holding their own.

They are most plentiful in Assam, where they are carefully protected.

A fine animal, the truculence of buffalo is often their undoing. They will often prefer a stand-up fight to running away even when unwounded, and when wounded are savage and determined enemies. They are usually hunted from elephants in Assam, and on foot in Central India. The latter is, of course, infinitely the finer sport.

THE OORIAL

(*Ovis vignei*)

VERNACULAR NAMES.—*Sha* or *Shapo*, Ladakh and Baltistan; *Oorin*, Astor; *Ps'h* (pl. *psyn'h*) and *Dumba*, Pashtu; *Oorial*, *Hoorial*, Punjabi; *Gud*, Baluchistan and Sind.

DESCRIPTION.—The typical oorial ram of the Punjab stands 32 or 33 inches at the shoulder, and these are the dimensions of the rams of the N.W. Frontier Province, Waziristan and Sind. The oorin of Astor is a little bigger, while the shapu rams of Ladakh reach 36 inches in height.

The oorial of every district except Ladakh are not to be distinguished, the Astor animal being much closer kin to that of the Punjab than to the Ladakh beast.

No reliance can possibly be placed on horn curvature, as this varies in individuals of every district and even herd. Horns of the "gud" from Sind and Baluchistan are usually more tightly curved and closer to the face, while those of Waziristan are more open, but this is by no means an unvarying rule, and I have shot two from the same hill-side, of which the horns of one curved in so that the points are directed inwards towards the face, while those of the other diverge outwards and away from the face. The same may be said of the shapu of Ladakh, and I have shot one with the points so much turned in that they had worn the hair from the angles of the jaw-bones.

The horns of Ladakh specimens can, however, be distinguished from those of other races by the rounding of the angles, and the corrugations being finer and closer.

The colour of all oorial is a light foxy red, but is more sandy in the Ladakh race. Most rams from the northern Punjab, though less usually in the Jhelam Salt range, have a saddle mark. This may be pied or (as in the specimen illustrated) black.

I have noticed that it seemed to be constant in herds, rams of the same herd having it the same colour, or entirely absent. This mark also occurs in most "gud" from Sind, but it is always black, and never pied, according to my observations. I had never seen or heard of this mark in shapu of Ladakh.

The Punjab oorial ram develops a fine beard and ruff in the winter; the beard may be pure white or grey, and the ruff black or dark grey. An old ram with a white beard and black ruff is a very handsome beast.

This beard and ruff is not so highly developed as a rule in trans-Indus rams, though I have seen good ones in Waziristan. In Astor it is not so well developed, and I have never seen any more than a very moderate development in shapu; though I have seen them in April, up to which month the ruff, if developed, should have been fully retained.

The general appearance of a typical oorial may be summed up as a sturdily built wild sheep of light foxy red colour, under parts white, as are the legs below the knee. The ram stands 32 inches at the shoulder and carries a well-developed ruff and beard, and has horns which are lightly corrugated and curving downward and forward, but rarely form more than three-quarters of a circle. The female stands 26 inches, has no ruff, and carries short upright horns about 7 inches in length.

The shapu differs from the above in being bigger, in having the angles of the horns more rounded, and the ruff almost absent, the beard being meagrely developed.

The best heads usually come from the northern Punjab, where a 30-inch head is common. A head of this size is exceptional in the Jhelam Salt range. Northern Punjab heads run up to 38 inches, but Waziristan has produced the biggest, mostly shot by men of the local levies: 41½ inches is recorded from here.

In Sind and Baluchistan a 28-inch head is considered good.

Thirty-inch heads are sometimes to be had in Astor and Baluchistan, and heads of this size are frequent in the Indus valley near Leh, where I have seen 37 inches from Stok nullah, and 39 inches has been recorded. Shapu horns are usually much more massive than oorial, and average 11½ inches in girth to the 10½ of the latter.

The rut takes place in October and November, one or two kids being born in the following April or May.

Distribution.—Typically, the Punjab from the Jhelam Salt range northwards. Also west of the Indus from Sind to the Attock Hills, and on both banks in Chilas, Astor and Gilgit. The very steep hills from Haramosh eastwards are unsuited to it, and it does not reappear until Skardo is reached. It is found in the Shigar valley and on both banks of the Shyok to ten miles above Khapalu, and there is a curiously isolated herd sixty miles higher up the Shyok on the left bank about ten miles below the first Buddhist village of Wanmaru. In the Indus valley it is found on both banks in suitable ground to about fifty miles above Leh, and also in the lower catchment area of the Zanskar river.

Habits and Characteristics.—The oorial provides some of the best sport in India, and now that its preservation has been taken in hand in several localities, it will remain for many years as a great asset to the Indian sporting world. They live in low broken hills, with a considerable amount of scrub as a rule, and stand great heat, but suffer much from drought occasionally, notably in 1920 and 1921 in the Punjab. They are wary, but the nature of the ground they live on usually makes the stalking fairly easy. Their eyesight is good and their scenting powers also, but their hearing seems indifferent. The old rams generally live in small bands of two or three to six, except in the rut. They feed early and late in the day, and do not shift much once they have settled down, except to seek shade. They graze mostly, but also browse on certain bushes. An absolute dearth of grass seems fatal to them however.

The shapu lives in a different type of country, affecting bare, open hill-sides, covered with gravel or shale. They are almost entirely grass-eaters, and are the most restless beasts. Time and again I have watched a herd settle down apparently for the day; then, half an hour later, an old ram will get up, stare around him, and begin to move slowly away. Others follow suit, and suddenly the whole herd will gallop madly downhill, stones flying and clouds of dust rising, cross the nullah at the bottom and then up the opposite slope, where they will lie down peacefully once more, to repeat the performance later on whenever it takes their fancy.

I was once debating how to get near a herd which was in an almost unapproachable position high above me, when they suddenly decided to shift, and passed within 150 yards of me, so that I bagged a good ram.

To judge a head the curve must be taken into consideration, also the drop of the horn. Some good shapu heads have little or no forward and upward curve, but consequently greater drop. Most "gud" from Sind and Baluchistan have much-curved horns, so that I have shot a 28-inch head which formed a complete circle.

Everywhere a 25-inch head is shootable, and 30 inches a good one.

Oorial are the blackbuck of the hills, and afford better and more sport than any other animal in India. Having hunted them in every district they inhabit and never failed to find good sport, I am grateful for their existence. Long may they flourish.

BHARAL

(*Ovis nahoor*)

VERNACULAR NAMES.—*Napu*, Ladakh ; *Bharal*, Gahrwal.

DESCRIPTION.—A very sturdily built sheep, of which the rams stand 34½ inches at the shoulder, and weigh 130 lb.; the ewes are about 4 inches smaller. The general colour is a blue-grey, the rams having a black throat and chest. The under parts and under surfaces of the legs are white. There is a black stripe down the front of each foreleg, and the tail is black. (No facial glands.)

The record head is 33 inches from near Gyantse, and anything over 25 inches is good. 23 inches is a shootable length in most districts, but in parts of the Shyok and in Zanskar many old rams fail to reach 22 inches.

DISTRIBUTION.—The bharal has a very wide distribution. Within the Indian Empire its westerly limit is marked by a few herds which wander into Hunza in the summer from the

Pamirs. It does not then reappear until the left bank of the Shyok, about forty miles below its junction with the Nubra. Its western limit on the Indus is the vicinity of Lamayuru (where I have shot one about five miles S.W. of the village), and is plentiful in Zanskar as far west as the Pense l pass. From these limits it extends right along the outer flank of the main Himalayan range, through Ladakh, Lahoul, Spiti, the Upper Sutlej and Gahrwal, to beyond Lhasa.

Habits and Characteristics.—The bharal lives at a higher average altitude than any other animal. The lowest that they come in Ladakh, as far as I have been able to ascertain, is 11,000 feet, and that only when the snowfall is exceptional. Their usual altitude in summer is about 16,000 feet, and I shot my best ram (a very massive 28¾-inch head) at 19,000 feet. They do not, however, go into bad ground except when alarmed.

They form large herds, and I have seen them up to the number of 200 from my tent door. Shootable heads are to be found with these big herds, but the very old rams are almost invariably apart in small bands, for which six seems a favourite number. They feed early and late, but a few will always be grazing.

Bharal are usually very hard to make out, owing to their colouring matching the blue shale and rock of the open hill-sides so closely. An approach should be made with great care, and the intervening ground studied closely for unseen animals. Often only a quarter of the herd is made out before beginning the stalk. The horns are also very difficult to judge, and they should be viewed from at least two angles, front and side, before estimating their length, while it is also a good thing to see them from behind so as to judge the inward turn of the points. Nearly all good heads turn inwards at the tips.

Bharal shooting is most exhilarating. The keen air, grand views, and the difficulty of finding and approaching a band of old rams, make it a most delightful method of spending one's leave.

The best districts I know of are in Lahoul and Northern Ladakh. I would strongly advise any one who wants good bharal heads to go over the Khardong Pass from Leh and march up the Shyok and Changchemmo river towards Tankse. It is

BHARAL. HORNS 24½ INCHES.

SHAPOO. LADAKH. RAM ON RIGHT, 29 INCHES.

To face page 120.

unfortunate that there is little else there, though fine ibex may be found, and snow leopard are plentiful. Snow leopard are the principal enemies of bharal, and live very largely on them. The rut is in October and November, and one or two kids are born in May.

An old bharal ram, with his smooth olive-green horns and jet-black chest, makes a very handsome trophy, and is a pleasant reminder of sport in the grandest surroundings.

SIND IBEX

(*Capra ægagrus*)

Vernacular Names.—*Sarah*, Sind; *Pasang*, Persia. (The male only is known as *Tehr* in Sind.)

Description.—This handsome goat stands 32 to 33 inches at the shoulder when fully adult, females about 26 inches. Females and young males are greyish rufous merging to white on the under parts. There is a black streak running the whole length of the spine, and an offshoot from it goes down each shoulder, like the stripes in the domestic donkey. The old males turn a very light grey, and can easily be distinguished from the others of their kind at a great distance, as they appear almost white. All males have a 6-inch chin-beard.

The horns are scimitar-like, and curve back with a wide sweep. They are very big for the size of the body, and care should be taken accordingly not to shoot an undersized beast. The record is 52½ inches, and anything over 40 inches is a good head. The points of an old buck's horns almost invariably begin to turn inwards, and I have a 43½-inch head of which the points actually cross.

Females carry small horns up to a foot in length.

Distribution.—This ibex is a dweller in low, hot hills up to about 5000 feet in height. Its habitat extends from the Khirthar range in Sind westward and northward right away to the Caucasus and the Taurus range in Asia Minor, wherever the ground suits them.

I have seen horns and skins from Sind, Mekran and the Taurus, and there seemed to be no great local variation, though the Persian and Caucasus beasts are a bit bigger.

Habits and Characteristics.—Sind ibex afford excellent sport and are very wary, while the difficult ground makes them well worth a trip. They are found in herds of five to one hundred in number, affect some of the worst ground at times, and have a trick of resting on the crest of a commanding ridge, with sentries on either flank, which is hard to circumvent. Occasionally old bucks are found alone ; they are then usually in very bad ground.

The heat, thorns, cactus, sharp-edged rocks and the usual absence of water make hunting them a fairly strenuous undertaking. It is best to bivouac out on the ground, or to allow for a couple of nights on the hill. Water must be carried up to the bivouac, sometimes from several miles away.

There can be no doubt that Sind ibex, in some parts of their eastern habitat, go without drinking for a year or more. It is to be presumed that they obtain the necessary moisture by eating fleshy-leaved plants, such as cacti or aloes, as do gazelle in Somaliland under similar circumstances.

Sind ibex are often driven in Mekran, but this is not a fair way of shooting them, as they provide such good stalking.

THE HIMALAYAN IBEX

(*Capra sibirica*)

Vernacular Names.—*Khel*, Kashmiri ; *Sakin*, Balti ; *Tangrol*, Kulu.

Description.—A big buck stands 40 inches at the shoulder and weighs 200 lb. They are thick-legged, stoutly built animals. Most specimens are set up to look much too slender ; the neck in particular, which has to carry the heavy horns, is usually made too thin.

The coat is thick and woolly in winter, and is shed in early summer, at which season ibex look very patchy and untidy. The colour is very variable, any shade from dark brown to coffee colour being found, or patches of light and dark brown, which make an animal look almost piebald. I have seen all shades in a big herd up the Shyok, but the light shade seems commoner there and the dark in Eastern Kashmir, but there is no definite rule. The coat is generally darker in summer than in winter. There is a chin-beard about 7 inches long.

The record horn for the Indian Empire is a 55-inch head from Gilgit. I know of two heads of over 50 inches shot in Baltistan since the Great War, and there are plenty of fine heads still left.

Lydekker has tried to define a number of local races, which are so obviously based on insufficient material and inaccurate geographical knowledge as to be quite untenable.

I have shot ibex in very many districts from Haramosh to Lahoul, and examined hundreds of heads and living animals, and can safely say that no definite rule can be laid down as to body colour, or as to curve, thickness and spread of horns, or the number, size or regularity of the transverse ridges.

The thickest heads I have seen have mostly come from the Wardwan, and those with the most numerous and regular transverse ridges from Padar, in the Chenab valley. I have, however, seen heads from the Saltoro valley (a tributary of the Shyok), which are identical in type with those from the Gonari nullah on the Kashmir-Chamba border.

Distribution.—Roughly, both sides of the Himalayas from Chitral to the Sutlej valley. Not in the Shamshibri, Kaj-i-Nag or Pir Panjal ranges, but on both banks of the Chenab from a little below Kishtwar town, up to its sources. Both banks of the Shyok throughout its course. The upper catchment areas of the Ravi and Beas, and the right bank of the Sutlej. There are no authentic specimens from south of the Sutlej. The Himalayan ibex rarely descends below 7000 feet, except in the Haramosh district in winter, and must have hill-tops of over 10,000 feet, to which it can ascend in summer.

Habits and Characteristics.—Ibex are lovers of cold, and are found at 12,000 feet even in winter. I have seen them above the Zogi-la at more than this height in early April, when there was deep snow for hundreds of miles around them. It is difficult to understand how such a big animal finds sustenance, but they seem to live by browsing on the twigs of small bushes, from which they scrape the snow with their feet, or knock it off with their horns. Many are killed by avalanches in the spring.

When the snow melts they feed greedily on the new grass,

sometimes throughout the day, and are then easier to approach than later in the season. I have seen a shootable buck feeding on a particularly luscious patch right down on the bank of the Hushe River in May at 8000 feet, and pay no attention to the shouts of my coolis from about 300 yards away. This was after a late and heavy fall of snow, which must have brought many of the ibex to a half-starving condition. They will usually feed up in the morning, then lie up in some commanding position during the hotter hours of the day, and then feed down in the evening, at the same time quenching their thirst at some small snow-water stream. During the night they will lie on some big knob, a tumbled mass of big rocks being a favourite spot. I have often seen this process reversed, however, the direction being down in the morning and upwards at night, but only early in the year.

Snow leopards are their principal enemies, and kill a great many.

Ibex are found in herds of every size up to 150. The biggest I have seen was 120 in the Hushe nullah in Baltistan. Old bucks will usually be found with the herds up to June, and after that they form small parties. I have seen parties of bucks in the spring, but rarely with good heads among them. The rut takes place in December, and the kids (one or two) are born in May.

The nature of the ground occupied by ibex varies very much in different districts. It is usually not very difficult, and calls for steady walking without real climbing; this is particularly so in Baltistan. In Kishtwar I have shot an ibex on ground so bad that after three and a half hours' hard climbing, during which my fingers got so cramped I had to sit for half an hour straightening them up before taking the shot, the buck whirled out into space on being shot, and did not touch anything for 700 feet, and then bounced another 400 feet. He was mush when I got down to him. A great disappointment, as he measured about 42½ inches, as near as I could judge by piecing a horn together, and that is a good head in that district.

They are very regular in their habits, and it is a comparatively easy business, after studying their habits for a couple of days, to intercept a herd on their way to or from their feeding-grounds, although it may entail a climb by moonlight.

Autumn shooting will generally entail a night's bivouac high up, so as to get within easy reach early in the morning.

They will generally run uphill, and the shot should be taken from a little above their level if possible. If taken from too much above they will bolt downhill and away, before going up.

The best heads are to be got in Baltistan, and there are many ibex left, and much ground which is very little shot over.

In Baltistan heads should average 40 inches or a bit more, but in the Wardwan and Chenab valley a couple of inches less. There are still a good number of 45-inch heads left in Baltistan, but 43 is as big as can be expected in their south-eastern habitat.

May and June are the best months everywhere for ibex shooting.

Patience is the chief virtue in securing good specimens. Good spying, a study of the habits of a herd and a careful approach, to which ample time is allotted, ought to give a couple of good heads to any man who can shoot straight at 150 yards.

MARKHOR

(*Capra falconeri*)

Vernacular Names.—*Markhor*, Hindostani and Pushtu; *Bum*, Astor and Gilgit; *Gharsa*, Pushtu; *Sarah* (also for Sind ibex), Baluchistan.

Description.—The markhor is divisible into several local races, on the score of size, coloration and shape of horns, but they are none of them sharply defined, except the markhor of the range which runs from a little south of Kohat to the Sheikh Budin massif, with a break south of Isa Khel.

The typical race comes from the Kaj-i-Nag range of Kashmir, and is usually known as the "Pir Panjal" variety, as it also extends into the Pir Panjal hills on the south, where markhor were first much shot by British sportsmen, owing to the accessibility of the ground. The horns of this race have a deep spiral but a straight axis, a big horn having two and a half to three complete turns. The record head (65¾ inches) is of this race, and came from the Mozi nullah in the Kaj-i-Nag in 1924. There are, however, not many markhor left of this type, as they are terribly poached, and steadily decreasing in numbers. This race also exists in the Shamshibri mountains and the middle Kishen Ganga valley.

This same type of horn is repeated in Chitral, but the Chitral head is usually thicker than the Kaj-i-Nag type.

In Astor and Gilgit is found the extreme type with a very wide divergence of the first turn above the head, the upper edges of this turn sometimes being almost in a straight line with each other, and at right angles to the head. The first turn is very large, and the typical horn has only two complete turns. This is usually the most massive type of horn. The record for this type is a 60¾-inch head shot in 1907 in the Gilgit district. Further up the Indus, in Baltistan, the heads are of a type between the Astor and Chitral, and are, to my mind, the handsomest of all. All the above horns are measured on the curve, along the keel which begins at the back of the base.

From Chitral as we go west and south, the axis of the horn becomes straighter and straighter, and the turns shallower, so that the horn becomes in Baluchistan more of a grooved rod than the stick of barley-sugar found in the Kurram. There are, of course, exceptions, especially in Baluchistan, where horns almost of the Kaj-i-Nag type turn up now and then; and in the Chiltan hills the horns are usually of this type. All these horns are measured straight. The best Baluchistan head recently shot is a 36¾-inch, shot by Lieut.-Col. Browse in 1925, and is, as far as I know, the best "straight-horned" head shot by a British sportsman. There are one or two bigger which have been brought in by Pathans, notably a 39¾-inch head from the Sufed Koh, now in the East India Club.

The male markhor is typically a fine heavily built goat, with a chin-beard when young, which merges into masses of long shaggy hair on the neck and shoulders. They stand, when adult, from 35 inches in the small Kohat race, and an inch or two bigger in Baluchistan, up to 42 inches in Astor. The colour of young bucks and ewes is light brown, turning in old bucks to dark grey. In straight-horned races the coat is short, but thick and crisp in winter, close and smooth in summer, while the hair of the neck and shoulders is never developed to more than a rather shaggy mass. The long coarse coat of the Himalayan races covers the whole body in winter, but in summer the hair is very much shorter. The Kohat-Sheikh Budin race is much squarer in build than the rather long-bodied Himalayan races, and I have never seen a horn varying from the very straight, shallow-grooved type. This race is rapidly being exterminated.

Distribution.—Locally from a little south of Quetta in Baluchistan right along the frontier hills, at any altitude between 2000 and 13,000 feet, through eastern Afghanistan, Chitral, the Swat valley, Buner, the Indus valley from a little below Skardu to thirty miles above Attock on the right bank. The middle Kishen Ganga valley, Shamshibri, Kaj-i-Nag and Pir Panjal mountains. It is not found in Ladakh, or east of these last-named three ranges.

Habits and Characteristics.—Markhor do not love snow, and come down low in winter, which unfortunately makes them very easy to poach, and they have had less benefit from protection than any animal in Kashmir. Some of the straight-horned races live in hot, low hills, where they cannot get higher than 4000 feet in summer.

They both browse and graze, feeding on young grass in spring and after rain, but they seem to live mostly on leaves of trees, such as hazel and birch.

The rut is in December in the Himalayas, and in late October and November with the straight-horned races, the kids, one or two in number, being born five months later.

Markhor, as a rule, live in very bad ground, and invariably have steep precipices near by on which they can take refuge. They have also the habit of hiding in clefts and patches of jungle, wet weather driving them into forest. They do not like open ground, and must at least have scrub jungle, while the Himalayan races prefer hill-sides with a certain number of trees about.

The highest I have seen markhor is about 13,500 feet in Haramosh in August, but when rain and mist began they all went down about 3000 feet and took to the jungle-covered cliffs, where they are very hard to find.

The markhor is, I think, the king of hill game. A fine beast carrying a grand trophy, he lives in very difficult ground and is hard to approach. They take their rest in the usual goat fashion in some commanding position, and usually descend morning and evening to feed. They sometimes lie down on their feeding-ground during the day.

The pace at which a herd will come down a hill to feed is amazing.

The herd may be up to forty or more strong, and old bucks are to be found with the herd at any time of the year, but, except during the rut, are more likely to be in small parties of three to six.

In Kashmir a shootable buck is over 45 inches, but heads of this size are hard to find now in the Kaj-i-Nag, while only one head over 42 inches has come from the Pir Panjal in the last twenty years. A 50-inch head, which is what is always aspired to, may turn up, but it is unlikely, and Astor and Baltistan are much more promising ground.

Gilgit and Chitral are closed to the ordinary sportsman, and available ground in Kashmir is dreadfully poached. A few permits (usually three) are issued every year for Chilas, and an occasional good head is to be got there.

The straight-horned races are hard to get anywhere. A 20-inch head (measured straight) is now considered shootable in Sheikh Budin, and 25 inches is good; the corresponding measurements in Baluchistan are 24 inches and 28 inches.

The ground which straight-horned markhor live in is particularly bad, and it is only this which has saved them from extermination at the hands of the armed tribesmen who hunt them. In Baluchistan a certain measure of protection has been accorded them, and they are safe for the time being, but elsewhere they are steadily disappearing. I have had three trips after the markhor of the Kohat hills, and consider that these hills are the worst I have been on. In addition to their steepness, the rock is crumbly and rotten.

Judging a markhor's head takes a lot of practice. The variation in the number of turns, the depth of the spiral, and the length straight have all to be considered. With the straight-horned markhor, only the last has to be taken into account, and is best judged by comparison with the length of the face.

THE HIMALAYAN TAHR
(*Hemitragus jemlahicus*)

VERNACULAR NAMES.—*Kras*, Kashmir; *Kurt*, Chamba and Kulu; *Jhula*, *Tahr*, Gahrwal.

DESCRIPTION.—A sturdily built goat, covered with masses of coarse, flowing hair, and with a fine ruff, the buck tahr stands about 38 inches at the shoulder and weighs about 180 lb. The horns are short and stout, curved sharply back and then inward in an old animal. They are ridged up to the last three inches of their length, and the front edge is strongly keeled. The record is 16¼ inches, but very few have been shot over 15 inches, and 14 inches is exceptional. Anything over 13 inches is a good head, and 11½ inches is shootable.

The colour of bucks is usually light brown (like the ewes) when young, growing darker with age, but this is by no means invariable. I have seen half a dozen old bucks together, and shot the two biggest with 13½- and 13¼-inch horns. One was light brown, and the other very dark brown. The other four were all darker than the biggest head. The face is always dark brown.

Females of this species have four mammæ, while the female Nigiri tahr has two.

The rut occurs in November and December, and one or two kids are born in May or June. I think, from the great number of tahr I have seen, that two is just as frequent as one, and do not agree with Lydekker on this point.

DISTRIBUTION.—The westerly limit of the tahr is the Pir Panjal range, where a few still remain; they are numerous at the bottom of the Wardwan valley, and particularly plentiful in the valley of the Chenab throughout Kishtwar. I have seen them in Bhoonjwar, and they are one of the principal objects of the big game hunter in Chamba. In Kulu and the Sutlej valley they have been greatly shot down, but a good many remain in Kumaon and Gahrwal, while their easterly limit seems to be in Bhutan. They do not cross the main Himalayan chain to the barren N.E. flanks.

Habits and Characteristics.—They inhabit quite the worst ground of any beast I have hunted, except, perhaps, the straight-horned markhor of the Kohat district. They demand a combination of big cliffs, rock and forest, which makes them hard to get at, not only on account of the difficulty of the climbing, but because they are usually invisible from any intermediate point of the stalk, and direction is very hard to keep.

They are plentiful in most parts of their habitat, and give as fine sport as any animal in the world. Unfortunately, many a good trophy is lost through falling hundreds of feet into a river, or to be smashed to fragments on the rocks. Tahr do not like snow and keep below it to as low as 5000 feet, then follow it up when it melts. In April I have seen 300 on the opposite slopes of the Chenab valley in Kishtwar when sitting down by the track up the left bank ; and there are places on the right bank where tahr are plentiful, yet their position is almost impregnable. Early in the year tahr may turn up in any place below the snow where a combination of rocky cliffs and forest is to be found. Old bucks are often solitary, and lie up in hollows under rocks or tree-roots in the middle of the day, but I have seen a party of sixteen old bucks, of which the smallest had horns over 12 inches, which always lay up on the crest and both sides of one of a series of knife-edged ridges which run up the side of the Chenab valley at a point where the ground is so bad that I believe it is impossible to get within range. Three to six is the usual size of a party of old bucks, and the size of the body is often a useful guide to the best head, as they seem to continue growing well after maturity. In judging the head, the length and downward curve of the points, above the ridged surface, is the true guide to a good head. Some very old bucks are almost black. Do not forget the masses of hair on a tahr when shooting at him, and aim low.

An old buck standing with all four feet together on a point of rock overhanging a thousand-foot drop, his long hair waving in the wind, and a general attitude of "You can't get near me" about him, is a fine sight, and a perpetual challenge to any right-minded big game hunter, which it is almost impossible not to take up.

I am always thankful he does not carry as fine a trophy as a markhor, for then he would be reduced through persecution, and good sport would suffer.

THE NILGIRI TAHR

(*Hemitragus hylocrius*)

Vernacular Name.—*Wari atu*, Tamil. The "ibex" of the S. India sportsman.

Description.—This animal is rather bigger than the Himalayan tahr, bucks standing 40 to 41 inches at the shoulder. The chief superficial difference is the all-round smoothness of the Nilgiri animal compared with the Himalayan. The coat is short and close, and the horns only lightly ringed and not keeled. There is no ruff. The general colour is brown in ewes and young bucks. Bucks turn dark brown with a black face, and develop a conspicuous light patch on the back behind the ribs, from which they have acquired the name of "saddleback" among big game hunters.

The record horns measure 17½ inches, and a good many have been shot measuring over 16 inches, but anything over 14 inches with a 9-inch basal girth can be considered a good head.

Distribution.—At one time tahr were terribly shot down in the Nilgiris, but rigid protection enabled them to recover and be once again open to very limited shooting. Now they have greatly increased of late years, and hords of fifty to sixty may once again be seen in favoured localities. In the Anamalai hills they never suffered so much and are fairly numerous, but in the Nelliampathi and Travancore hills they have been badly poached and reduced in numbers.

Habits and Distribution.—These tahr are not nearly so partial to bad ground as the Himalayan species, but nevertheless like to have it within easy reach as a refuge, and are perfectly at home on it.

They are usually to be found on hills with plenty of open

grass slopes, and big cliffs, at 4000 to 7000 feet. They come up to feed on the easy slopes in the morning and evening, and retire to more difficult ground to rest.

The rut appears to occur throughout the cold weather, and usually one kid is born. But kids may be dropped at any time of the year; old bucks are found either alone or (more frequently) in small parties, or with the herds. In January and February, however, I have rarely seen the old "saddle-backs" with the herds. They provide good sport, though not as fine as the Himalayan species, and sometimes have to be followed into really bad ground. As a rule the chief difficulty is the wind, which is very variable, and mist in the winter months.

It is exhilarating sport on the grassy uplands of the Nilgiris on a crisp winter morning, and some wonderful scenery can be admired, to enhance the enjoyment, on the great cliffs which scarp the edge of the mountains above the plains. The variety to be shot is also great, as bison and sambhar may be seen within a few hundred yards of the tahr ground, and tiger have occasionally turned up on the cliffs themselves. Leopard are the chief enemies of the tahr, and may be met with at any time.

It is the only real mountain shooting of Southern India, and so the difficulties and dangers have been somewhat exaggerated by some writers, but nevertheless the sport is worthy of attention by even the most hardened frequenter of the Himalayas, and adds charming variety to jungle shooting.

In an interesting note on Nilgiri tahr by Mr. A. P. Kinloch, in the Journal of the Bombay Natural History Society, No. 2 of vol. xxxi., he remarks on their extreme reluctance to enter jungle in the Nelliampathis. This is curious, as I have twice seen them lying down in jungle in the Nilgiris.

THE SEROW

Capricornis sumatrensis)

VERNACULAR NAMES.—*Ramu*, Kashmir; *Goa*, Chamba; *Yanu*, *Kulu*, *Tehr*, Nepal; *Taw-seik*, Burma.

DESCRIPTION.—Standing 38 to 40 inches at the shoulder, the serow appears a clumsy mixture of donkey, goat and

SEROW GROUND. LATE AUTUMN.

SEROW GROUND. EARLY SPRING.

To face page 132.

antelope. The general colour of the coarse shaggy coat is black, and there is a considerable stiff mane on the neck and withers. The coat may be more or less grizzled, and the black shades into ferruginous red on the flanks and lower thighs and shoulders, and again turns to dirty grey on the inside of the limbs and the belly. There are usually white markings about the lower lip, throat and chest, which vary individually in extent and occurrence. The same race of serow inhabits Kashmir and the Himalayas as far as Nepal, from which country I have recently examined specimens. Further east the rufous seems to increase, and in Assam and Arakan there is regular rufous colour-phase, which extends as far as the Ruby Mines district of Upper Burma, though both north and south of it the black is the usual form.

Individuals from the Salween valley, Tenasserim and W. Siam all seem to have a curious purplish tinge like the bloom on a damson. It is possible these represent a separate race or species, as also may the Bhutan-Assam serow. Sufficient material has not been obtained to work them out yet. I have examined nearly thirty specimens covering ground from Kashmir to Naini Tal, and two recent specimens from Nepal, but my experience of the large remaining area of their habitat is confined to four specimens. I do not include the numerous horns which I have seen in Burma and Malaya. They tell us nothing.

The horns are black, ringed up to the basal third, and curve backward and downwards, diverging slightly from the parallel. The biggest head known is 12¾ inches from Gahrwal. In Kashmir the biggest head recorded in the Game Records is one of 9¾ inches (6½ at the base) shot by me. East of Gahrwal, throughout Assam and Burma, horns again are smaller, and 9½ inches is the best of a great many I have measured. Both sexes carry horns, and the best head of a female I have seen is a very thick 8¾ inches shot by me in Kashmir. The sexes are very hard to distinguish, an old male appearing bulkier in body, but as they are seldom seen clear of forest, it is only very occasionally any comparison can be made.

Distribution.—From W. Kashmir along the Himalayas through Burma to Malaya and Siam.

Habits and Characteristics.—Serow are most difficult beasts to hunt, as they are seldom seen away from a combination of crag and jungle, whence they only emerge to graze in the shadow of a cliff in some secluded ravine in the Himalayas. They seem to favour some particular elevation between 6000 and 9000 feet, and will not leave it even in heavy snow.

In October 1923 I saw a female serow with a kid of the year lying in thick snow on a ridge for several hours. Four or five may be found on the one hill-side, but as a rule they live solitary, except for a mother and young one, though I have once seen three together.

The rut is in the end of October, and the young one (usually the only one) is born in early June or late May.

I once saw an old buck courting, and it was a curious sight. He chased the lady up and down and round a cliff about 200 feet high, his forelegs moving stiffly together so that his feet made a curious clacking noise, either on the rocks or hitting together. At the same time he uttered loud grunts. Three times the chase was dropped and again renewed, until finally he cornered the lady in a gully between a big rock and a chestnut tree. He then set about butting her in most ungallant fashion, banging her violently against the rock, until she submitted to his attentions.

To get a Himalayan serow, first find where they live ; then watch the shady parts of the cliffs in the early morning and evening. Very often the first indications seen are two vertical white lines, which are the inside of a serow's legs.

In the Salween valley and Tenasserim they have a trick of depositing their droppings in the same place for weeks on end, and this is taken advantage of by the native hunter. There they usually inhabit the serrated rocky tops of the ridges which crop out of the jungle.

Serow are sometimes driven, and invariably bolt downhill. They will turn on their pursuers at times, and attack both dogs and men, even when unwounded. One of a pair has been known to attack a hunter who had killed its mate. They can cause considerable damage.

They utter a weird braying scream when wounded.

THE HIMALAYAN GOURAL
(*Nemorhædus goral*)

VERNACULAR NAMES.—*Goral*, W. Kashmir ; *Pij*, E. Kashmir and Chamba ; *Rain* (nasal), Punjab and Jhelum valley.

DESCRIPTION.—Goural stand 28 inches at the shoulder on an average, and are stockily built. The general colour varies a good deal. Females and young males are usually light brown suffused with grey, while older animals lose the brown and turn dark grey. They all have a white patch on the throat and a dark (not always black) dorsal stripe, the outer side of each leg being black. I have shot goural from W. Kashmir to the Siwaliks, and seen specimens from other districts down to Tenasserim. The general characteristic of a darker coat in the old buck seems constant. The skins of three bucks of different ages shot on the same hill-side in W. Kashmir in 1926 show this characteristic very strongly, and it is certainly constant in the Chenab valley and Punjab.

Horns.—The horns are black, ringed for the basal third, then smooth, and taper to a sharp point. They curve back and diverge slightly as a rule. They are present in both sexes. Record is 9¼ inches ; anything over 7 inches is good.

I consider that there is insufficient evidence to establish two species of Himalayan goural, and that the above description applies to all goural as far east as Bhutan.

DISTRIBUTION.—In 1906 a goural was washed down the Swat River in a flood and cast up dead near Chakdara. I take the Swat River to be their north-western limit. They then extend south-eastwards all along the south side of the Himalayan range, and may be found from the lowest foothills up to 8000 feet, wherever there is combination of trees, grass and rocky cliffs. They appear to be indifferent to heat, but do not like snow.

The easternmost limit of the Himalayan goural would appear to be Bhutan. Skins from Assam show decided differences, and are evidently related to the Burmese animal.

HABITS AND CHARACTERISTICS.—The goural provides delightful sport within easy reach of many hill stations, and many a novice has obtained his first useful experience hunting them. They prefer very steep, grassy hill-sides, with a certain amount of scrub jungle, but must have bad ground to retire to when alarmed. They are never very far from patches of forest, to which they retire in bad weather.

Old bucks are usually solitary, but may be found with others in small parties. Nine is the most I have seen together. As a rule several will be found on the same hill-side.

They have a wonderful capacity for hiding, and it is amazing how, as the sinking sun gets off an apparently barren hill-side, six or seven goural will appear from nowhere, grazing on different parts of it. I once sat down to lunch in a valley in Kishtwar, and had been there over half an hour, when I put up my glasses to test them after cleaning. It happened that I looked at a big rock about eighty yards away on the opposite slope, which has a vertical crack about a foot wide down the centre. Inside this crack I saw a goural standing.

I sent a man round to bolt the buck, and it stayed there until he was within a couple of yards, then jumped out and made off downhill, but was bagged.

The one illustrated, a 7¾-inch head, lived on a cliff above my camp, and had defeated me several times. He used to appear grazing in a grassy hollow near the top of the cliff. I would then cross a small nullah and get into the dead ground at the base of the cliff (which was about 800 feet high), and climb up a line by which he could not possibly see or wind me, yet when I reached the point overlooking his pasture, he was always gone.

I was striking camp on my last morning when he appeared again, but this time I left the shikari behind with the glasses, while I went forward. Just after I had got out of sight in the dead ground, the shikari whistled and brought me back. As soon as the buck could no longer see me, he had walked down the cliff about twenty yards and gone into a hole under a big boulder. The position was such that I could not possibly have got a shot by going up to him myself, so I sent the tiffin cooli, who actually climbed on to the boulder and poked the little beast with his khud stick before he bolted out and came down the cliff like a bouncing cricket-ball. I had remained sitting on a rock below, and smashed his spine with my second shot, so that he came whirling out and landed on his tail in the nullah with such force that his thighs were broken and the back of his skull driven in.

It is hard to distinguish the females from the males, but the females are lighter in colour, and usually in company with one or two others. The horns of a female are thinner than the buck's, and do not reach 6 inches as a rule.

They all have a sharp, hissing note of alarm.

Goural are very fond of sunning themselves after rain and in cold weather, and may then be seen standing on the crest of steep-sided spurs or isolated crags.

I can strongly recommend goural-shooting as a sport. They are many, and live in ground that needs care and a steady head, while the mark is a small one to shoot at.

The surroundings are pleasant, and it is an excellent preliminary to tackling markhor or tahr.

Goural are quite good eating, and are most useful for the pot, as supplies are scarce in most of the country they affect.

THE BURMESE GOURAL

(*Nemorhædus evansi*)

This goural is about the same size and build as the Himalayan species, but has no dorsal stripe, while the legs are black behind and rufous-yellow in front. The usual colour in Burma seems to be dark grey suffused with brown; but I have seen two skins from Assam of a very yellow shade, and another from the Salween valley of the same type. They are distributed from Assam and Arakan to Western Siam in suitable country, which postulates big hills with big cliffs and very heavy forest, which are usually hard of access, while the size of the trophy has not made it worth while to most to undertake their pursuit. Consequently information about them is very scanty and hard to obtain. I only know of them personally in Tenasserim and on the Meping-Meklong divide in Siam, and my material and information is much too exiguous to pronounce as to species and habits.

Goural on the western borders of Assam and from Nepal usually have a strong red-brown tint.

THE TAKIN

(*Budorcas taxicolor*)

VERNACULAR NAME.—*Takin*, Mishmi hills.

DESCRIPTION.—A thick-legged, stumpy animal with humped withers, the takin is coloured smoky brown, darker on the legs and face, and lighter on the back. The coat is long and coarse.

The horns are curiously shaped, curving downwards and outwards, then straight up. The bases of the horns are set close together. The record is 23 inches.

The bridge of the nose is much curved.

The height at the shoulder is about 43 inches.

DISTRIBUTION.—At elevations between 7000 and 13,000 feet from Bhutan to N.E. Burma.

HABITS AND CHARACTERISTICS.—This strange beast has affinities with the serows and antelopes, and has only become really known in the last twenty years. They inhabit jungle-covered mountains on and about the snow-line, and like rough ground with occasional cliffs. They live in small herds, up to about twenty-five strong, as a rule, but bulls are to be found solitary or in small parties of two to four or five.

They will charge fiercely when wounded, and the natives say they will also do so when unwounded. Of late years they have been shot by British sportsmen in the Mishmi hills and also in N.E. Burma, but their habitat is at present very difficult of access.

THE NILGAI

(*Boselaphus tragocamelus*)

VERNACULAR NAMES.—*Nilgai*, Hindostani; *Roz* or *Roj*, Punjabi; *Guraya*, Gond; *Kard-kadrai*, S. India.

DESCRIPTION.—This large antelope is an uncouth brute, with wretched horns for its size, for they only run up to 10 inches in length, while the bulls average about 55 inches at the shoulder. The cows are some 4 inches less, and are hornless.

The cows and young bulls are a dull khaki colour, and the old bulls turn a deep iron-grey, which darkens with age. The old bulls are usually striped with white on the withers, and also have patches and spots of white on the face, throat, chest and fetlock. The bulls have a pendant tuft of coarse hair on the throat.

DISTRIBUTION.—Nilgai occur throughout India in suitable country; they are unknown in Burma and Ceylon. In India they occur from the extreme south northwards as far as the Ravi and northern Rajputana. Lydekker states that they are particularly common round Jhelum, but in the course of much travelling in that district I have never seen or heard of one, and I doubt their reaching the Chenab river. They are addicted to a mixture of jungle and cultivation, and are not to be found in very heavy forest.

HABITS AND CHARACTERISTICS.—Where plentiful, as in the southern Punjab, nilgai do a great deal of damage to the crops, cutting up with their feet what they do not eat.

In spite of the average sportsman's distaste for shooting such ugly, semi-equine-looking beasts, which provide such a poor trophy, the usual limit of a specimen or two should be exceeded. The cultivator suffers so much from their depredations that his goodwill is gained by shooting them, and useful work done.

It is best to stick to the vernacular name of "roj" in the north, and its equivalent in the south, so as to avoid the word nilgai, and the possibility of wounding the feelings of Hindus by the supposed connection of these beasts with the sacred cow.

Nilgai skins make good leather, and their marrow bones are good eating.

THE FOUR-HORNED ANTELOPE

(*Tetraceros quadricornis*)

VERNACULAR NAMES.—*Chousingha*, Hindostani; *Ban-bakri*, Central India.

DESCRIPTION.—Standing about 24 inches, the chousingha is a slenderly built, gazelle-like animal. The colour is light brown, and the face-markings of the gazelle are wanting, while the ears are more rounded. The spike-like horns are upright and smooth, the back pair arising from the usual place, the front and shorter pair from just above the eyes. The maximum for the back pair is 4½ inches, and 2½ for the front pair. In S. India the front pair are usually not developed. The posterior horns are about 2½ inches long at eighteen months old, but the anterior pair are not developed until the third year.

DISTRIBUTION.—Rajputana and the United Provinces southwards throughout Peninsular India. Not in Assam or Burma.

HABITS AND CHARACTERISTICS.—The chousingha is a solitary little beast as a rule, but occasionally found in twos and threes. Low rocky hills and the flat grassy tops of ridges in the forest are their usual haunts, and they are not much shot, being usually met with when larger game is being hunted.

They are sometimes captured and make pleasant pets, not developing the pugnacious dispositions of other deer and antelope.

They are fair eating.

THE BLACKBUCK OR INDIAN ANTELOPE
(*Antilope cervicapra*)

VERNACULAR NAMES.—*Kala hiran*, Hindostani; *Mirg*, Punjabi; *Keliman*, Tamil.

DESCRIPTION.—Standing 32 inches at the shoulder, an old buck is coloured black on the back, sides and outside of the legs, and white on the throat, chest, belly and inside of the legs. There is a sprinkling of buff along the spine, which increases with age on the nape of the neck. The face is black, with a large white patch round the eye, the inside and bases of ears and the lips and chin being white.

The black colour is to a certain degree seasonal, turning brownish in the hot weather, when a number of bucks seem to lose the black altogether in Central and Southern India. Some bucks seem never to turn black, and this is more prevalent in Central India than in the north; though I saw, in November 1919, a big herd in Patiala, which contained at least half a dozen bucks carrying horns over 22 inches in length, and there

BLACKBUCK. HORNS 27½ INCHES.

A MIXED BAG IN THE PUNJAB.

To face page [illegible]

was not a single black one in the herd. The black colour has no reference to the rut.

Young bucks and does have the white marking much the same, but are khaki-sandy coloured where the old buck is black. Young bucks seem to begin turning darker about their third year as a rule, but are not mature until their sixth year.

The horns are very handsome with their graceful spiral turns and annulations. Except for the Sind ibex, I know of no other animal which carries such large horns in proportion to its size. The best head known is one of 31¾ inches, killed in Jind and in the possession of H.H. the Maharajah of Jind. I have seen this fine head, which has a tip-to-tip measurement of 29 inches.

I have seen one other head, which just topped 30 inches, and four or five over 28 inches, which is the measurement of my own best. Nearly all heads over 27 inches are from the Punjab, and I have bagged eight heads over 25½ inches in Patiala. The heads grow steadily smaller the further south these antelope live, and though an occasional 25-inch head is killed in one or two very favoured localities in Central India, anything over 22 inches is good, and 20 inches is scarce in Madras.

Distribution.—Throughout Peninsular India in the plains, and as far north as the Bikanir desert and the Chenab river. Not in forest or very wet climates, so absent from Assam and much of Bengal.

Habits and Characteristics.—Blackbuck are to be found in enormous herds over 500 strong in the Punjab native states, and over 1000 strong in Bikanir. I counted up to 400 in one herd in Patiala in January 1926, and that was not more than three-quarters of the total. They do an immense amount of damage to the crops in such places, especially to young grain and wheat. It cannot be expected, therefore, that the ryot will refrain from shooting them under the circumstances. In northern Rajputana the big herds seem to feed more in waste lands than they do further east. Old bucks will often be found a little apart from the herds, while one curious feature is the occurrence of parties, up to twenty in number, composed of young bucks approaching maturity, or old broken-horned animals which have been turned out of a herd. They fight fiercely, and fatalities sometimes occur. Some tribes make use of this characteristic to catch blackbuck: letting a tame buck out to fight a wild one, first covering the tame one's horns with nooses, so that the two buck are entangled. A tame buck is also often used as a decoy, to bring a wild one up to a hidden shikari.

The rut lasts throughout the cold weather, and, in fact, it may occur locally at any time but the hot weather. It is most frequently at its height about March and April. An old master buck is a great tyrant, pursuing does and turning them back into the herd with the points of his horns, strutting round stiff-legged uttering loud challenging grunts, and quite intolerant of the presence of any other buck which shows signs of approaching maturity.

Blackbuck undoubtedly do not drink at all for months on end in some parts of India, but it cannot be said for certain that they are altogether independent of water.

Their leaping powers are amazing, as is their speed. There is no authentic account of a blackbuck being ridden down or caught by dogs, if unhampered in any way by a wound or soft soil. Their trick of bounding high in the air when a herd is moving away in open country, and when leaping over each other in full flight, is astounding; but it becomes amazing when they pass through a small patch of millet 7 feet high, and they appear a couple of feet clear of the top of the crop. They have a curious way of giving a series of short, stiff-legged bounds when a herd is preparing to clear off.

Blackbuck have provided more good sport, and introduced more men to the pleasures of big game shooting, than any other animal. They are wary, even when numerous and preserved, while, where they are much shot, they can give as fine a morning's stalking as any game animal in the world. I do not consider that wearing native clothes or using a cart are fair ways of getting up to them. It is always possible to outwit them, and the greater the difficulty the better the sport.

Great care should be taken when after buck that no human

beings are in line with the shot, and a bullet which breaks up easily should be used.

Light weapons of the rook-rifle type, however, are quite unsuitable for shooting buck. It is perfectly true that they are to be killed with these, but a great many go off wounded to die in great pain. I once saw a railway officer fire several shots from a trolly on the line out of a 300-bore rook rifle at a buck, which went off obviously hit. Later in the morning I jumped this buck about two miles from the place where he had fired at it, and, after a great deal of trouble, succeeded in killing it. It had three bullets in it, only one of which had gone through, while the remaining two were lodged in its stomach, with hardly any trace of expansion. The unfortunate buck would probably have taken two or three days to die.

The photo showing a living buck was obtained under curious circumstances in Hissar. I saw him lying down about five yards from the bank of a canal feeder at sunrise, on the side away from the sun. Getting into the water, I managed to reach a point just opposite him, and, pushing the camera carefully over the top of the bank, snapped him. He then bolted, and I shot him when he stopped to look back from about 130 yards away. His horns measured 22¾ inches, and by comparing them with the length of the face, a good basis for estimating heads may be arrived at.

THE TIBETAN ANTELOPE OR CHIRU

(*Pantholops hodgsoni*)

VERNACULAR NAME.—*Chiru*, Ladakhi.

DESCRIPTION.—A quaint-looking antelope, with slender forward-curving horns (transversely ridged on the front face), a swollen, hairy muzzle and thick soft coat, the chiru stands about the same height as the blackbuck, 32 inches at the shoulder. The upper and outer parts are pale brown, and the lower inner surfaces white. The face is black, also the front of the legs.

Horns.—Record 28½ inches, a good head 24 inches. Females are hornless.

The skin is extraordinarily thin, and tears like paper.

DISTRIBUTION.—This antelope is only found within the

Indian Empire a little to the east of the Karakorum Pass and in the Changchemmo valley of Ladakh. It has a wide range further east and south in Tibetan territory.

Habits and Characteristics.—The chiru has a curious appearance, and equally curious habits. They are rarely found in herds, but single ones and parties of two or three may be seen dotted about at small intervals on the undulating gravelly ground on which they are usually found. They graze on the grass and small plants which grow close to the ground on the wind-swept Tibetan plains, and migrate over considerable distances in search of them.

They are much afflicted by the grubs of a parasitic fly, which burrow under the skin of the quarters, and it is a curious sight to see them suddenly begin jumping about from side to side, then scour over the plain to get rid of their tormentors.

The old bucks have a habit of scraping shallow pits for themselves, and lie in these with just the top of the head and the horns visible. It is consequently often very difficult to pick them up with the glasses, especially as mirage is very prevalent on the ground they inhabit. They may be found grazing at almost any hour of the day.

They have good eyesight, but poor noses.

I have never heard of their coming below 12,000 feet.

THE GOA or TIBETAN GAZELLE

(*Gazella picticaudata*)

Vernacular Name.—*Goa*, Ladakh and Tibet.

Description.—A slender, light sandy-grey gazelle, standing 24 inches at the shoulder, it has no dark markings except a black tip to the tail. There is a white disc on the buttocks, and the under parts are white. The coat is long and fine, rather sparse in summer but thick in winter. The horns, of which the record pair measured 15¼ inches, are very closely ringed with an almost right-angled backward bend at the last quarter, the tips again turning upwards. Twelve inches is a good head.

Distribution.—The goa's westerly limit is the Rupshu district of Ladakh on the left bank of the Indus; it does not occur on the right bank in the Indian Empire. It is found in Tibetan territory further up the Indus towards Gortak, in the Upper Brahmaputra valley above Lhasa and near Gyantse.

It is a hardy little animal with wonderful eyesight, good hearing, and practically no sense of smell. I have stalked to within twenty-five yards of them with the wind blowing straight to them.

They usually live in small bands of three to seven (the most I have seen together is nine) in very open ground, and their wonderful eyesight, and the help of that ubiquitous nuisance the Kiang, make them decidedly hard to approach.

In snowy winters, which are infrequent on the Tibetan plateau, they suffer much from wolves, as their feet cut deep into the snow, while the wolves traverse it easily. Lynx probably account for some of the young ones, but snow leopards are never found on the same ground.

They are very good eating, when hung for a week or ten days, as is easy to do in Rupshu.

THE SEISTAN GAZELLE

(*Gazella seistanica*)

Vernacular Name.—*Ahu*, Seistan and Western Sind.

Description.—Very like the chinkara in size and general appearance, but with less brown on the face, and with horns distinctly lyre-shaped and incurved at the points. They are also more heavily ringed than those of the chinkara.

Distribution.—I have taken this to be the gazelle of Seistan, Western Baluchistan and Sind, which was formerly called the Persian gazelle.

I have never shot them myself, but have seen a few heads, which are remarkably like those of Persian gazelle, obtained in Irak.

I have seen gazelle in Sind on both sides of the Khirtbar range, which may be Seistan gazelle, Kennion's gazelle or chinkara. The matter is very interesting, and should be cleared up.

In the Seistan gazelle the females have no horns, but the females of both the other species are horned.

THE INDIAN GAZELLE OR CHINKARA
(*Gazella bennetti*)

VERNACULAR NAMES.—*Chikara* or *Chinkara*, Hindostani; *Husai*, Pushtu; *Ahu*, Sind; *Kalipi*, Central India.

DESCRIPTION.—Bucks average 26 inches at the shoulder and weigh 50 to 55 lb. Does are about 4 inches less in height.

The general colour is sandy red, which is darker where it meets the white of the under parts. The chin and chest are white. The tail is very dark brown; likewise the knees. The bridge of the nose is dark brown, and so are the sides of the face, the eyes being set in a light patch.

Both sexes carry horns, those of the buck being of the usual gazelle type, with the points as a rule divergent. I have shot chinkara near Peshawar, and seen heads from there and the Derajat, whose horns were distinctly lyrate in curve when viewed from the front. It is a long time since I got my own specimens of this type, and they were lost during the war, while I have failed to obtain any more. It seems possible that the trans-Indus chinkara is a distinct race or species. The best buck horns I have seen were slightly over 16 inches, shot by an Indian officer of the 14th Sikhs near Ferozepore a good many years ago. My own best is 14⅝ inches from Patiala. Nearly all the big heads come from the north of India, and nothing under 13 inches can be considered good there, while 12 inches is a very good head in Central and Southern India.

The Maharajah of Cutch has shot some fine heads in his state of over 15 inches.

The biggest female horns I have heard of is a 9-inch pair from the Campbellpore district. The horns of a female are thin, almost smooth, and curve very slightly.

DISTRIBUTION.—All over the plains of India, wherever there is open country. They do not go into forest, but are fond of scrub jungle, sand-hills and gravelly plains cut up with ravines. I have seen them on the right bank of the Indus from Peshawar and the foot of the Buner hills all the way down to Karachi, and as far towards the Afghan frontier as the Dardoni plain in the Tochi valley.

HABITS AND CHARACTERISTICS.—The chinkara is a restless little animal, fond of broken ground. They are usually to be found in small herds of five to eight, but I once saw twenty-three together on the Bikanir border. The old bucks are often found solitary, particularly among sand-hills, where they have a trick of scooping themselves a hollow to lie in on the shady side.

The constant wagging of the chinkara's tail is a curious habit, which is perhaps caused by the attentions of parasitic flies. The skin of the lower half of the back is often full of the grubs of these flies, and a chinkara will often go through curious antics trying to dislodge them. The skin of the one mounted in the Prince of Wales Museum at Bombay, and which was shot by me in Hissar, looked, on being held up to the light, as if a charge of B.B.'s had been fired through it, but there is no trace to be detected now that the skin is cured, either in this or many other similar specimens which I have acquired. Blackbuck are not affected with these grubs.

Shooting chinkara is great fun, and the little beasts are usually hard to get up to, and provide a very small mark to shoot at. One usually begins by jumping them, but they seldom run very far, and it is often possible to get cover immediately and follow them up. Very often patient walking, always as if you are going to pass 200 yards to a flank, will obtain a shot. They will trot away at first, but gradually get more confidence as to your intentions when a slight alteration of direction will obtain a shot at 170 to 180 yards. The shot will have to be taken standing, as sitting down will send the gazelle off immediately.

Chinkara eat very freely of gourds, melons and cucumbers in the Punjab fields, and cause a good deal of damage in young grain and wheat. They do not seem to be nearly as pugnacious as blackbuck, but become very dangerous in captivity. I have seen several albinos ; the last I saw was caught near Mianwali in 1924, and was quite tame. I also saw one at Hissar in 1921.

Chinkara go up to 4000 feet in the Punjab Salt range, where I have shot them on the tops of the steepest hills, and seen them feeding amongst a herd of oorial. They frequently keep company with blackbuck.

THE KASHMIR STAG

(*Cervus cashmiriensis*)

VERNACULAR NAMES.—*Barasingh*, Hindostani ; *Hangul*, Kashmiri ; *Changul*, Pahari.

This is the " barasingh " of many sportsmen and most natives of N. India. Kashmiri shikaris use this name when speaking to Europeans.

" Barasingh " is also used by both natives and Europeans in referring to the swamp deer.

DESCRIPTION.—This grand stag stands about 52 inches at the shoulder, and is generally brown, varying from light bay to dark sepia : sometimes distinctly grizzled. It is darker on the back and neck and down the outside of the legs, the brown fading to dingy white on the inside of the limbs, under parts and buttocks. Fawns are spotted to their third year.

Hinds stand 42 inches at the shoulder.

The colour of stags fades a good deal in summer, but from October onwards the bigger stags are usually very dark, and their coats often look as if they had been watered, they are so sleek and glossy.

Horns.—Five is the normal number of points on each horn, but I have seen a fifteen- and several fourteen-pointers : that is counting only true points, and not " snags " or " offers ".

The bez is usually longer than the brow, but the trez may be longer than either. I have measured trez tines of over 18 inches in length.

The record head for length shot in recent years was 51¾ inches. It was a straggly, uncouth head of eleven points. I have seen two others of over 50 inches in the last five years (since 1921), both of them " royals " (*i.e.* carrying six points on each horn) ; one came from the Sind valley, and the other from a poacher's hut, probably obtained in the Tral rukh. My own best was a 47-inch ten-pointer, with very heavy beam.

I expect the record to be passed any day, judging from living specimens I saw in the Dachgam rukh.

In estimating a trophy, length is by no means the only criterion. Girth, weight, symmetry, and number and strength of points, all go to make a good head. I consider that the royal illustrated is a very good head, although 5 inches shorter than my big ten-pointer. I shot this royal in the Liddar valley after many days' hunting. He was a woodland stag, and never came into the open.

The horns are usually shed in March, the older stags losing theirs first, but some of the smaller stags may retain them up to the second week in April.

Distribution.—The hills bordering the Kashmir valley, except the Pir Panjal, and southwards to the borders of Chamba State.

Habits and Characteristics.—The "call" of a Kashmir stag varies from a shrill squeal to a resonant blare, while a big stag lying down will often utter a deep moan. A small stag's call is often no more than a whistle. It is always better to go for the deeper note.

Calling does not usually begin until the end of September, and varies very much in vigour. In some years stags seem hardly to call at all. After heavy rain or an early fall of snow most stags will call. In September 1905 I was camped at about 10,000 feet in a valley to the south-east of Islamabad, and we had 101 hours' continuous rain, resulting in very heavy floods in the Kashmir valley. It ended at 7 A.M. on September 4, and within five minutes of it ceasing, four stags began to call vigorously in the valley below me, continuing for about half an hour. I did not hear another call for six weeks.

After shedding their horns the stags follow the melting snow up to the top of the tree-line, and, when their horns are well grown and in velvet, leave the forest for the open hill-tops. When the horns have hardened they descend again into the trees about September 1, and rub them clean, gradually working down to about 9000 feet, at which level they usually join the hinds at the beginning of October. The height of the rut is about October 20.

There is no westward migration in the spring. The stags are wont to move over to the western slopes, which are more thickly wooded as a rule in Kashmir, but they remain well distributed all over the high ground of the Kashmir valley throughout the summer, and I have met with them all along it from May to August. I have even watched stags travelling steadily westwards in early October.

They are grazing animals as a rule, coming out morning and evening from the forest, but in winter they are forced to browse after the heavy snow has fallen.

The grazing in spring largely governs the quality of the heads in the autumn.

Many good stags never leave the forest, and, to my mind, give the finest sport of all.

The usual method of hunting is to start very early up the hill, and be in position at sunrise on top of a ridge commanding the favourite feeding-grounds. Then watch for a stag to emerge, or wait for a call. If nothing turns up, then wait all day for stag to come out in the evening. This is the popular method with the Kashmiri shikari, and as a rule he will employ no other. But do not be satisfied with this, but go into the forest and try for a stag there as well. There are certain nullahs where the finest stags seem never to leave the forest, and are hardly ever with hinds. They will call, though infrequently and not very loudly. These are the beasts to go for. A combination of listening and tracking will locate their favourite haunts, and then quiet moving and a keen look out in the early morning will eventually give a shot.

Whatever method is adopted, the hunting of the Kashmir stag is one of the most delightful pursuits imaginable. The climate and scenery are glorious; the ground is by no means difficult; and the stag provides a grand trophy as a subsequent reminder of a real good time.

THE SHOU OR SIKKIM STAG

(*Cervus affinis*)

VERNACULAR NAME.—*Shou*, Bhotia.

Very little information is to be had about this fine animal, and, as far as I can ascertain, it has only been shot by two British sportsmen.

The horns run to 56 inches, carrying five points a side, and are noticeable for the heaviness of the beam. The brow and bez tine are noticeably depressed, and in all heads I have seen their tips turn sharply up and are set close together.

The only first-hand description I have had stated that the stag was a dark sepia brown, with a very large yellowish rump patch.

Shou are found in the borders of Sikkim and Bhutan, in the Chumbi valley, and the hills on each side of the Brahmaputra valley east of Lhasa.

THOROLD'S DEER

(*Cervus albirostris*)

Horns of this deer may turn up, though it is very unlikely that the animal itself will be encountered by an Englishman.

The antlers are like those of a Kashmir stag without the bez tine, and have the beam suddenly bent back at the middle. The brow-tine is a good way above the burr. The top inner tine is set immediately behind the other, and not level with it as in most Kashmir stags.

The animal itself has a white muzzle, and a curious reversal of the hair on the withers. It is at present only known from Tibet.

THE SAMBHAR

(*Cervus unicolor*)

VERNACULAR NAMES.—*Sambhar*, Hindostani; *Mahar*, Terai; *Jerao*, Himalayas; *Dhank*, C.P.; *Kadvi*, Canara; *Kad'mai*, Tamil; *Sat*, Burma.

DESCRIPTION.—There is only one species of sambhar in the Indian Empire, which varies considerably in size. About 52 inches seems to be the average height in their northern habitat, 54 to 55 in the central parts of India (Dunbar Brander records one of 59), and again 52 inches further south. They seem to decrease steadily in size the further south they live from Assam through Burma, and, while stags I have shot in Upper Burma reached 50 inches at the shoulder, two with exceptionally big horns for the district, shot in Tenasserim and Western Siam, were each only 48 inches.

They are usually a dark sepia brown in the cold weather, shading into yellowish under the chin, throat, thighs and tail. They are usually greyish or light brown in the hot weather, but these shades are also frequently seen in the cold weather.

Old stags are usually very dark, almost black.

They are heavily maned, and have a long, very coarse coat. The ears are particularly large.

The horns are of the simple rucervine type, carrying a brow tine and two tops formed by the bifurcation of the beam. They are subject to curious abnormalities, such as a bifurcation of all the top points. The specimen illustrated has a bifurcated brow tine, which is unusual. Basal snags are not common, but I have seen a head from Karenni in Burma which had several large ones on each horn.

The record horn is a 50⅛, shot in Bhopal, and 48¼ is the next longest recorded. I have seen both these fine heads. Any head over 40 inches is a good one, but this length is not likely to be met with outside the Central Provinces. A 35-inch head is a good one in the Nilgiris or N. Rajputana, while a 28-inch head is good in Burma. The most massive heads usually come from Burma or Northern Bengal. I measured a 30-inch head from Baxa Duars which had a mid-beam girth of 9 inches.

Many Burma heads are far from massive, however, and it cannot be considered a constant characteristic. The best head I have measured in Burma was 34½ inches.

The relative lengths of brow tine and beam vary very greatly. I have seen a 32-inch head from the United Provinces which had 21-inch brow tines.

The relative lengths of the inner and outer top tines is also very variable, and Dunbar Brander has an excellent plate in his *Game Animals of Central India* illustrating this point.

Distribution.—The northern limit of the sambhar is Jaipur State, where a few are still to be found in the rocky hills which crop up from the plains on the south-eastern edge of the Bikanir desert.

At about the same level they are found at the foot of the Himalayas, and from these points southwards throughout India, Burma and Malaya, wherever there is suitable ground.

They prefer hills, and go to a height of 9000 feet in the United Provinces, but are also to be found in alluvial plains, where there is extensive cover.

HABITS AND CHARACTERISTICS.—The horns are usually shed at the beginning of April and are clear by the middle of October. This is by no means a regular rule however. I have seen big stags in hard horn in Canara in July, and in Burma at the beginning of August; while Fletcher, in *Sport in the Nilgiris*, records seeing stags in full horn in August and September. This, of course, makes it possible that some stags carry their horns for more than one year. Dunbar Brander definitely states that there is no evidence of this ever occurring in the Central Provinces, so there is evidently considerable local variation in this respect.

In some districts sambhar suffer from a curious disease known as " sore neck ". This starts with a raw-spot the size of a shilling at the bottom of the throat where a whorl of hair is found. The area round the spot loses all hair, the spot increases to the size of half a crown, and the naked area may eventually include the whole neck.

I have never seen this disease in animals from Rajputana, the United Provinces or the Nilgiris, nor in the Zoos at Karachi and Bombay. I have seen it in Canara, slightly, and the Calcutta Zoo, occasionally. Dunbar Brander states that it occurs, but not commonly, in the Central Provinces, and that he has only noticed it in the hot weather and early rains, so that he associates it with the new growth of hair.

Evans in *Big Game Shooting in Upper Burma* states that it is universal in Burma, and offers to " eat his hat " if any of his readers shoot a stag in Burma which is not so affected. I am afraid he would have had to tackle this indigestible meal if he had been with me in June 1914, for I shot an old stag in the dry zone of Upper Burma which showed no trace of it. It is the only one of four I have shot in Burma and W. Siam which has not had it, and every other sambhar, male or female, of the many I have seen at close quarters in the forests of that area has appeared to suffer from it. It would seem to be caused by a parasite which flourishes in moist heat.

Sambhar are both grazing and browsing animals. In the Nilgiris they seem to graze mostly, but in Burma the reverse seems the case. They also eat many jungle fruits, and such fallen flowers as those of the mohwa, and, in Burma, of the cotton-tree. These last are also eaten by barking deer, and I have seen both animals feeding under the same tree in Lower Burma. They are destructive to trees, barking them both for food and in the process of clearing their horns. On one long hill-top on the Burma-Siam border, there were a large number of a whitish soft-barked tree growing in mixed forest; not a single one of these seemed to have escaped being barked by sambhar all round for about two feet at an average height of four feet from the ground.

They are fond of bathing and wallowing, especially old stags, and one evening I saw three of the latter in wallows at about 7000 feet in the Nilgiris in January, where it froze hard every night. Small rain-water pools on ridge-tops are very good finds for them in Upper Burma during hot weather.

The stags are very pugnacious, and their fights seem to have little or no relation to the rutting season, which is shortly after the horns are clear. I have seen stags fighting fiercely in February and March, the rut having finished over two months before. They seem to fight for a particular bit of ground. An old stag seems to join the hinds for a few days only in the rut, and soon drives off any young intruder.

The period of gestation is said to be eight months, and one or two fawns are born.

Sambhar are never found in large herds; eight hinds and one or two young stags is the most I have seen together, and four or five hinds are the usual number, while old stags are solitary.

Sambhar have many enemies—men, tigers, panthers and wild dogs all hunting them—so they have developed their defensive powers to a very high extent. They have fine hearing and good noses, though poor eyesight, and are very hard to get up to, thus providing great sport for the still-hunter.

They are difficult to drive, marvels at finding a weak spot and most determined in breaking back. I have three times known a man killed by a stag, which declined to go forward,

MALAYAN SAMBHAR KILLED IN RIVER.

MALAYAN SAMBHAR HEAD. HORNS 29 INCHES.

To face page 154.

the last case occurring in September 1926 near Jhansi. I once saw a stag tree every one of twenty-five beaters in a Nilgiri "shola", and then trot back up to the top of the next hill and watch where we went to next.

I think a "silent" beat is most effective with them.

Once in the Salween valley, I saw a stag come up early in a beat and bush in under some fallen bamboos within twenty-five yards of me. When the beaters and dogs came up to him, he burst out and went back, knocking over two dogs.

It is in the Nilgiris that I have had the prettiest sport with sambhar. On a frosty January morning they may be spotted feeding just outside a "shola" and stalked from a long way off. The slightest suspicion aroused and they are back inside the cover. The tops of the Central Indian hills are the best finds for good trophies, and any open space should be approached with great care, and the edges thoroughly examined: an old stag has a great trick of standing just inside the edge of the forest.

All sambhar have a loud, metallic, warning bell, and the stags challenge with a sort of screaming bellow. In the Nilgiris, I was once still-hunting by the full moon on the edge of a tea estate, where sambhar do a great deal of damage to the tea. I had spotted a stag some eighty yards away uphill of me and crept carefully up the edge of the forest to try and get against the light. He had evidently moved back inside the cover, for suddenly his screaming challenge was uttered within three or four yards, which so startled me that I jumped away and fell plumb into the 6-foot ditch dug round the estate to keep out elephants.

THE CHITAL OR SPOTTED DEER

(*Cervus axis*)

VERNACULAR NAMES.—*Chital*, Hindostani; *Jhank*, Northern United Provinces; *Jati*, Canarese; *Paliman*, Tamil.

DESCRIPTION.—A beautiful animal, the stags standing 36 inches at the shoulder, the chital is very gracefully built. The coat is a light chestnut freely spotted with white. The ground colour fades to reddish khaki in the summer, and cured skins also lose the chestnut shade. The throat and under parts are white, and the long tail is heavily fringed with white.

The horns, which carry the usual six points, vary a good deal in shape. Most rise fairly upright from the head without any great spread, but some diverge rapidly, the beam going out a long way before rising vertically, and do not approach at the tops. The upper tine is on the inside of the beam and about a third of the way down it. A 40-inch head has still to be recorded, but I have seen one of 39¾ inches, and know of two of ¼ inch less. They vary in length with locality. A 34-inch head would be good anywhere, but 31 inches would be the equivalent in Coimbatore or Canara.

Distribution.—Throughout Peninsular India, as far north as Khansdesh on the west, and extending up to the confines of Jammu on the north-east. It is absent from Assam and Burma.

Habits and Characteristics.—This handsome and sporting deer is seldom to be found in thick cover, but likes open forest and undulating ground. It feeds freely in grassy plains with occasional patches of jungle, and makes some raids into the crops, which may carry it two or three miles from its usual haunts.

They are fond of water, and the banks of rivers are their favourite ground. One of the most beautiful sights I have seen was a herd of about fifty chital in giant bamboo jungle on the bank of the Kalinadi river in North Canara. It was just after a heavy shower of rain, and the sunlight falling in long shafts through the glittering bamboo fronds on to the dappled hides of the herd, with the shining river as a background, made a picture very pleasant to recall.

The horns are usually clear of velvet in January and are shed in August, but this varies greatly with locality. I have seen a herd of about a hundred in the Pathri Dun at the end of March, which contained stags carrying horns in every stage of growth.

Chital are usually gregarious, and herds up to 500 strong have been reported, but parties of all sizes may be met with.

The rutting stag has a loud and harsh braying call.

CHITAL. WIDE HORNS 33½ INCHES.

CHITAL. NARROW HORNS 34½ INCHES.

To face page 156.

THE HOG DEER

(*Cervus porcinus*)

VERNACULAR NAMES.—*Para*, Hindostani; *Day-ay*, Burmese.

DESCRIPTION.—Standing about 25 inches at the shoulder, this little deer is sturdily built; while its long body, and the carriage of its head, make the English name very applicable to its appearance.

The colour is a dark brown in winter, paler in summer, when it acquires a number of white spots on the body. In Burma these spots are nearly always present.

The under parts are pale, and the inside of the ears and the under side of the tail are white.

The horns are of the simple rusine type, with three points, and run up to 25 inches in length in Burma, where a 19-inch head is good. In India they are much smaller, 21 inches being the maximum recorded, and 16 inches a good head.

DISTRIBUTION.—This species has rather a curious distribution, as it is found on the islands of the Indus river below Dera Ismail Khan; and, up to 1920 at least, there were a few higher up, but they seem to have been shot out. As far as I have been able to ascertain, it does not again turn up until the high grass of the Dun and the Ganges valley is reached. It is general through the latter. It is not found in Peninsular India or Assam, but is common in Burma along the valleys of the main rivers, and may turn up in any patch of swamp down to the south of Tenasserim. It extends into Siam.

HABITS AND CHARACTERISTICS.—A dweller in thick cover and high grass, it is not usually possible to shoot these little beasts without beating for them. "Walking them up" on an elephant is good fun, and calls for quick and accurate shooting; as, in very high grass, they usually abandon their scuttling mode of running for a series of immense bounds for the first fifty yards or so, so that they have to be taken "on the wing".

When beaten out into open country, they give an easy shot, as they stop frequently to look round.

They are often ridden and speared in the Ganges Kadir and one or two other places.

THE SWAMP DEER OR BARASINGHA

(*Cervus duvanceli*)

VERNACULAR NAMES.—*Barasingha*, Hindostani ; *Gond*, United Provinces ; *Gaoni*, Central India ; *Bhilwa*, Assam.

DESCRIPTION.—This very handsome stag stands about 54 inches at the shoulder, is brown in colour, merging to yellowish on the under parts. As in most Indian deer, they become lighter in the hot weather. Hinds are lighter coloured than stags as a rule. The young are spotted.

The horns are in general form like the sambhar's, extra points being formed by the bifurcation and re-bifurcation of the top tines, while small points and snags are often carried on the upper tines, which remind one forcibly that this deer is intermediate in type to the sambhar and thamin.

The record head is 42 inches, and 35 is a good length ; but girth, symmetry, spread and number of points all go to make a good trophy.

DISTRIBUTION.—The Eastern Terai and Northern United Provinces, Western Assam and Northern Bengal. Locally in the southern and eastern districts of Central India.

Lydekker states that it occurs in Sind, and gives a "Sindhi" name for it. I have been quite unable to discover any foundation for this. It may have existed very many years ago in the Indus valley in company with the hog deer, but I cannot help thinking that it has been confused with the smaller animal. I have made many inquiries, but have always met with negative replies on the subject of its existence there.

HABITS AND CHARACTERISTICS.—The swamp deer is only a swamp dweller in the northern portions of its habitat, where water and high grass seem essential to its existence ; they are there mostly shot in beats or off an elephant.

In the Central Provinces they affect fairly open forest with grassy maidans on which they feed ; and, though they like water for bathing, it is not an absolute necessity. They do not go into the hills, but stick to the plains wherever they live.

The horns are clear by the beginning of November and are

shed in mid-April as a rule. The rut continues throughout this period.

Old stags usually rut early and leave the herds, which are at their biggest in December, and, like thamin, go off in small parties to live alone. The oldest stags are usually solitary.

The stags have a resounding challenge, which resembles a musical, metallic braying, commencing very loud and continuing diminuendo until the necessary breath seems exhausted.

THAMIN OR BROW-ANTLERED DEER

(*Rucervus eldi*)

VERNACULAR NAMES.—*Thamnin*, Burmese ; *Sangnai*, Manipur.

DESCRIPTION.—The general body colour is sepia brown, fading to light brown below. There is usually some white on the throat and about the muzzle and eyes. Occasionally a few white spots on the back. Hinds incline to be lighter in colour. The stag stands 44 inches, and hinds 41 inches at the shoulder. The coat is very coarse and rather sparse. The general colour is lighter throughout in summer.

Horns.—The horns are set on the long narrow head at right angles to the coronet, and the curve of the brow tine is continuous with that of the beam. The brow tine may reach 18 inches in length. The beam curves backward and outward, then sharply forward and inward. In old stags the bend forward makes a distinct angle in the beam, the curve being more continuous in young stags. There is usually a subterminal tine on the upper side of the beam, and several small points and snags between it and the tip. The end of the horn may be flattened or slightly palmated, but true palmation is only frequent among heads from S.E. Siam.

There are often small basal snags at the junction of beam and brow tine.

The record head is 42 inches, and anything over 36 inches is good. The length of the brow tine is also a factor in assessing a trophy.

HUNTING.—In Manipur thamin frequent grassy swamps, and poles are carried by which the shikari may ascend to spy, having stuck the end into the soft surface. The thamin there wear away the hair from their pasterns, and acquire splay feet, which prevent them sinking in too far.

Further south, in Burma, they are usually to be found in undulating ground covered with open jungle, between the foothills and the main rivers. In Siam they seem to take to swamp life again.

They are very fond of wallowing, and the stags are most pugnacious, many being found blind of an eye when shot. This is probably due to the position of the brow tine. I once shot a stag which was entirely blind in both eyes.

Horns are clear of velvet in January, and are shed in June in Manipur, late August or early September in Burma.

The best month for hunting is February, as the old stags are still with the herds, and the leaves have begun to fall. Later the bigger stags retire into the thicker jungle in small parties.

Very pretty stalking is to be had with thamin, and the trophy is handsome and peculiar. There are still a good many left in the haunts some distance from river or railway, but terrible slaughter has been carried out in the more accessible places ; while in the vicinity of oil-wells, the American employees have almost wiped them out for a radius of forty miles or more, such districts as Magwe, previously an excellent ground, being now empty of them, but for an occasional one.

Much unfair hunting has been carried out from carts. The thamin are accustomed to seeing the Burmans constantly driving carts through their feeding-grounds, and pay little attention to them. The lazy brute who takes target practice from these ought to be thoroughly ashamed of himself. No objection can be made to using a cart to take one out to the ground in hot weather, and it is useful for bringing back a stag, but shooting from them is plain murder.

Walk quietly and be on the ground early ; also be prepared to take all shots standing at ranges up to two hundred yards. Thamin heads are not easy to judge at first, and a decision has often to be made, and a shot taken, as the stag stands for a few seconds in an opening in the jungle.

BARKING DEER OR RIB-FACED DEER
(*Muntiacus muntjak*)

VERNACULAR NAMES.—*Kakur*, Hindostani; *Bherki*, Gond; *Jangli Bekri*, S. India; *Gyi*, Burmese.

DESCRIPTION.—Standing 21 to 25 inches at the shoulder, this little deer is sturdily built, with rather a long body. The colour varies from bright golden or foxy red to a golden brown, while very dark, melanistic specimens are not uncommon.

The horns are of simple type, the points much turned in and down as a rule, even hooked in some cases, and carry one small inner brow tine. They reach a maximum length of 7 inches in India, and are usually under 6 inches, but may run to 9½ inches in Burma. I have shot them up to 8½ inches in the dry zone.

The horns are borne on bony pedicles covered with hairy skin up to the burr, and from 2½ to 5 inches in length. These pedicles continue down the face to beyond the eyes, giving a curious appearance, from which the name of "rib-faced deer" arises.

A black line runs down the inside of the horn-pedicles, and down the face to merge into a dark brown patch. The outside of the legs is darker than the body, but the chin, chest and inside of the legs are white, as is the under surface of the tail.

Fawns are spotted, as very often the adults are in Burma.

The upper canine teeth are about an inch long in bucks, projecting well below the lip, and very sharp. Severe wounds are inflicted with these weapons in fights between bucks, or even on a dog.

In very old bucks the horns sometimes take a peculiar form. They lose the brow tine and become a simple spike, of which the upper inch or more is ivory white. These are never shed, and I have seen them used very effectively against a dog on one occasion. I have shot three specimens of this type in Upper Burma and Siam, and they are also recorded from the Himalayan foothills.

The horns are shed in May in Burma.

M

DISTRIBUTION.—The barking deer has a very wide distribution, as it ranges from W. Kashmir through the outer Himalayan hills, and E. Rajputana, then generally southwards in any forest country throughout Peninsular India and Assam, Burma and Malaya. The Burma and Malaya specimens average considerably larger than Indian, both in horn and body.

They may be found at any elevation up to 7000 feet, at which height I once shot one in the Chenab valley.

HABITS AND CHARACTERISTICS.—The loud bark of this little animal more usually reveals his presence than the sight of him, as they stick to fairly thick cover as a rule, and the only time they are to be seen in the open is occasionally emerging in the early morning or evening to feed in some isolated fields in the forest. Even then they stick to the edge and never venture far out into the open. The great length of tongue is an extraordinary feature, and it is well worth watching them when browsing in scrub jungle; they seem to wrap the tongue round the end of a leafy twig and pull the leaves into the mouth in a bunch, stripping the twig bare.

They are dainty feeders and movers, fond of trotting along jungle paths, when they often make a curious clicking or rattling noise whose origin is obscure.

When alarmed they give a series of ringing barks, which carry a very long way. They will often keep these up as long as the object of their suspicion is in view or hearing, and it is often possible, by leaving a man to move about gently in front of them, to slip round and get an easy broadside shot, guided by the barks. When come on suddenly they will bolt, uttering a series of short staccato barks, and the white flag of the under surface of the tail bobbing up and down as they clear the bushes.

They are solitary little beasts as a rule, and I have never seen more than three together, while they have many enemies, and form a favourite prey of pythons, in addition to carnivora.

They pair at different times of the year according to district. February and March is usual in Northern and Central India, October and November in parts of Burma. The period of gestation is apparently four months, one or two young being born.

The stags have a curious squealing bark which they utter during the rut. This is often imitated in Burma by blowing on a leaf, and the stag called up and shot.

They are not much sought after, however, and their preference for thick jungle and nocturnal habits preserve them in most places.

They are driven in some places, notably the Nilgiris, where they are called "jungle sheep", and used to be killed with shot. An unsporting practice, which led to many getting away wounded, and is now forbidden.

They lie very close, and I have walked within five yards of one lying close under a fallen log without his moving, thinking that I had not seen him. On getting out of sight I walked back fifty yards to his position to see if he had stayed, but he had slipped away.

They are very good eating, and afford pleasant sport where they are plentiful. Quiet walking and a study of their habits will give shots which are a useful education for tackling bigger game.

THE TENASSERIM OR FEA'S MUNTJAC

(*Muntiacus feae*)

VERNACULAR NAME.—*Gyi*, Burmese.

DESCRIPTION AND DISTRIBUTION.—A chocolate-coloured barking deer, with a bright yellow face, this little animal lives in the Tenasserim hills, Mergui and W. Siam.

I have seen it on the Ta'ok plateau in Tenasserim.

It may also dwell further north in the hills on the left bank of the Salween, and curiously coloured, dark barking deer skins have come from there and the vicinity of Bhamo, which may be of this species, or colour phases of the ordinary barking deer, or even a separate species.

There is still much zoological work to be done in this region.

THE MUSK DEER

(*Moschus moschiferus*)

VERNACULAR NAMES.—*Kastura*, Hindostani ; *Roos*, Kashmiri ; *Baina*, Gahrwal.

DESCRIPTION.—A quaint little beast, standing up to 24 inches at the shoulder, and 26 at the quarters, but most specimens are 2 or 3 inches smaller than this.

They are covered with a very dense coat of thick pithy hair, which acts as a protection from the great cold of winter, but is so brittle as to make the skin difficult to preserve.

This coarse coat makes them look clumsy and heavy, but I have seen them very active on bad markhor ground in Haramosh.

The ears are large and rounded.

The general colour is a golden or greyish brown with thick pepper-and-salt specklings. The shade varies a great deal in individuals.

The false hoofs are greatly elongated and hollowed underneath, so that they act as a snow-shoe in soft snow and prevent the animal sinking in.

The tail is very short.

The buck is armed with a pair of long upper canine teeth, which may project downwards as much as 3 inches from the jaw. He also has an abdominal musk-pod, from which he takes his name, and which is the cause of his never-ending persecution at the hands of the natives.

DISTRIBUTION.—From Gilgit southwards throughout the Himalayas, between 7000 and 13,000 feet, wherever there is forest and scrub jungle. It is not to be found in barren countries such as Ladakh and Zanskar, but has a wide range throughout the eastern half of Asia.

HABITS AND CHARACTERISTICS.—The musk deer is a solitary little beast which sticks to thick cover as a rule, and, when found, is usually confiding and easily shot. I have had one feed up to within a yard of my feet.

I have seen many in different parts of the Himalayas, but have shot only one, and that under rather curious circumstances.

One spring in eastern Kashmir, I had watched a big black bear into his midday resting-place under the base of an overhanging pine, and stalked the place. I had got within 100 yards of the bear, and was among masses of frozen snow held up in immense ledges by the pine trees, when I caught sight of a musk deer standing on the brink of one of these ledges about eighty yards above me. I wanted one specimen, so, seeing through the glasses that it was a male with a good pair of teeth, I shot him. As he rolled down almost to my feet, out rushed the bear, and my second cartridge accounted for him also. A rather unique "right and left".

MOUSEDEER OR CHEVROTAINS

THE INDIAN MOUSEDEER

(*Tragulus meminna*)

THE MALAY MOUSEDEER

(*Tragulus affinis*)

VERNACULAR NAMES.—*Pisura*, Hindostani; *Pisai*, W. India; *Kanchil*, Malay.

DESCRIPTION.—These tiny little animals may be met with while shooting, though they are hardly "big game".

The Indian species is about 10 inches at the shoulder, and yellowish brown in colour.

The Malay species is a couple of inches bigger, and more rufous.

The Indian species is marked with horizontal lines of white spots merging into stripes, the Malay is more heavily spotted and striped.

They are hornless, and the bucks develop very sharp upper canine teeth about ¾ inch long, with which they fight fiercely.

DISTRIBUTION.—Peninsular India as far north as Khandesh, Southern United Provinces and Orissa.

HABITS AND CHARACTERISTICS.—Little is known about these little animals. Those I have met with in India I have generally turned out of grass and rocks among hills. In Tenasserim I have two or three times seen them come out of evergreen jungle into a stream-bed in the evening, have a drink and then browse along the foot of the bank.

THE INDIAN WILD PIG

(*Sus cristatus*)

VERNACULAR NAMES.—*Sur*, Hindostani ; *Wet*, Burmese ; *Bura*, Korku ; *Paddi*, Gond ; *Kardupani*, Tamil. (Mohammedans in Northern and Central India will usually call wild pig "Bad janwar" or "bura janwar", meaning "bad animal" ; or in the Punjab simply "zinawar", meaning "the animal". Thus they avoid defiling their tongues with the name of the unclean beast).

DESCRIPTION.—The pig is too well known to need a detailed description. Sow and young boars are usually brown, old boars turning grey, but forest pig are usually darker than those of scrub jungle and open country. The race I have shot in Tenasserim and W. Siam is black, and seems more heavily crested than the average Indian pig. In Upper Burma they exactly resemble Indian specimens. The biggest pig recorded stood 39 inches at the shoulder, and was shot in Kashmir, but 33 inches is a big pig. I saw one in the Canara jungles which stood higher than some chital which were close to it, and must have been over 36 inches.

I have seen a good many tusks of 9 inches, but 10 inches is about the maximum, though bigger ones up to 14¾ inches (malformed) have been recorded.

The 39-inch pig shot in Kashmir by Rajah Amar Singh, and mentioned above, is reported to have weighed 600 lb., but this seems so enormous that there was probably some mistake made. A very big pig will weigh 300 lb., and one 34½-inch boar I shot in N. Rajputana certainly weighed that. Native weights made it a little over 320 lb.

DISTRIBUTION.—The Indian Empire up to 8000 feet.

HABITS AND CHARACTERISTICS.—Of course *the* way to kill a pig is with a spear from a horse, and pig-sticking is quite one of the finest sports in the world. There is, however, comparatively little ground where this can be done or tent-clubs organised ;

and the immense damage done by pig in nearly every part of India demands that they should be shot wherever there is no tent-club to deal with them.

Acres of crops are rooted up and destroyed, sugar-cane suffering particularly badly in the Punjab, and the lordly way in which an old pig will take up his residence in thick crops and refuse to quit for weeks on end, is remarkable. They also eat carrion, reptiles and molluscs.

Pig will associate in sounders up to 200 in number, but are commonly found in smaller numbers, about fifteen to forty being usual. Old boars may be found at any time with sounders, and breeding goes on throughout the year, though there is a distinct spring rut. The period of gestation is about four months. The young are born striped.

Sows make big nests of grass, in which the entire family live.

The courage and truculence of wild boar is notorious, and I have twice suffered from it in Canara by coming on an old boar when getting up to a bull bison I was tracking. In each case it was the early rains and the old brute got up out of a wallow, looked at me for about half a minute and then charged, so that I was forced to shoot, and lost my bison. One boar was 33 inches and the other 34 inches, so, judging by these and the very big boar previously mentioned as seen there, I should judge the N. Canara pig to average very big.

Hunting pig with dogs on foot and with a spear is very fine sport. It is wonderful what pluck a village pi will show, and I saw a bitch in a pack I got together in the Nilgiris, hang on to the ear of an old boar and get dragged fifty or sixty yards without letting go. Unfortunately the plucky dogs get very cut about, and camping out with them always ends in losing some through leopards.

In N. Rajputana, where the low rocky hills are divided by flat valleys about 300 yards across, pig are hunted with a combination of spear and rifle. They are there very numerous, but there is not sufficient good ground to admit of their being regularly ridden, and catching them as they dash from one hill to another is the only hope with a spear. Crops are scanty there and the pig get more than their share, so kill them as you can is the practice.

In Burma pig are not so plentiful, and are a good deal hunted for their meat, so stick much more to the forest. They do not seem to run nearly as big as Indian pig.

The pig is certainly one of the cleverest wild animals, and it takes care and a study of his ways to drive him successfully. More than with any other animal (except the sambhar) does the principle apply of driving him where he wants to go. A break back is a certainty, if he is forced in the wrong direction.

THE INDIAN LION
(*Felis leo*)

VERNACULAR NAMES.—*Sher*, *Baba sher*, Hindostani ; *Oontia-bagh*, Guzerat ; *Sawach*, Kathiawar.

DESCRIPTION.—It is unnecessary to give a description of the Indian lion, which in no way differs from the African animal. It used to be stated that the Indian lion is maneless, but it has just as fine a mane as the African. It is much the same size.

DISTRIBUTION.—The Indian lion was at one time found over a great part of Central India, but has not been seen there for over sixty years. One was killed near Jhansi in 1926, but it was almost certainly one of the African animals, turned down some years before by the Maharajah of Gwalior, and of which one or two, or their descendants, still survive.

The lion is now restricted in India to the Gir Jungles in Kathiawar, though an occasional individual has been known to stray into neighbouring districts.

HABITS AND CHARACTERISTICS.—They have the same characteristics as the African lion, but live more on domesticated animals, owing to the scarcity of game. They show as bold a front when they are infrequently shot at a party given in honour of some great man, and are as liable to take up man-killing instead of cattle-killing.

As they are carefully protected they will probably survive for many years, but can scarcely be considered as forming a part of the normal big game fauna of India.

THE TIGER

(*Felis tigris*)

Vernacular Names.—*Sher*, *bagh*, Hindostani; *Pillai*, S. India; *Kya*, Burmese.

Description.—No detailed description of the tiger is necessary, but there are one or two points on which comment may be made. The frill round the jaws is usually much more highly developed in cold climates, and the hair on the neck almost develops into a mane in some northern specimens, such as is never found in examples from Burma.

The colour is usually redder in S. Burma than elsewhere, though this must not be taken as a constant rule.

As regards size, a tiger will measure up to 44 inches at the shoulder, while 10 feet straight in total length is a very big specimen anywhere.

The length of the tail varies by as much as 15 inches, and the body-length and bulk is a greater factor in assessing a good trophy.

The size of tigers has been the subject of a great deal of controversy. Either by personal inquiry or from their writings, I have investigated the dimensions of tigers shot or seen killed by the following noted sportsmen: Colonel Pollock, General Mackenzie, the brothers Hadfield, Digby Davies, Colonel A. E. Ward, Sir John Hewitt, Dunbar Brander.

They account between them for over 1600 tigers from every part of India, and the biggest recorded is 10 feet 7½ inches, while under thirty are over 10 feet. This is straight measurement between pegs. Measuring over the curves adds another 5 inches. A pegged out skin will tape 1½ to 2 feet more than the straight measurement, and a dressed skin 12 to 16 inches more, according to whether a good breadth has been tried for or not when pegging out.

Now where are all the big tigers of over 11 and 12 feet talked and written about in previous days? Many of the tigers noted above came from jungles untouched by previous shikaris, and where the quantity of natural food would make it probable that there, if anywhere, would be found the monsters of olden days.

There can be no doubt that these huge tigers were inaccurately measured, or else recorded under the magnifying influence of a long sitting over claret and madeira to celebrate the day's sport.

There seems to be little difference in the average size of tigers, except in Burma, where they undoubtedly tend to go smaller towards the south ; more very big tigers seem to come from the foot of the Himalayas than elsewhere.

A tigress has been measured (Sir John Hewitt) 9 feet 6 inches, but the average is 8 feet 3 inches.

Tigers vary very little in their markings, the full complement of stripes being born with the cub, and these separate out with the expansion of the body. I once shot a tigress in Upper Burma which was deficient of the full number of stripes on the shoulders and ribs.

There is a race of white tigers living in Rewa State, and one has recently been presented to H.M. the King by the Maharajah of Rewa and mounted in the Natural History Museum at South Kensington, while I have also seen one (October 1926) sent to the Bombay Natural History Society, but unfortunately in too poor condition for mounting. In albinistic specimens the stripes are faint on a heavy white ground.

There is no absolutely reliable evidence of the occurrence of a *black tiger*.

Distribution.—Throughout Peninsular and Central India to N.E. Rajputana and North-East U.P. on the north, an occasional tiger wanders along the foot of the Himalayas as far as the Sutlej valley. They have been known to go to 9000 feet in the Himalayas. Then throughout Assam and Burma to Malaya.

Habits and Characteristics.—There has been a great deal of tiger literature produced by casual hunters, and also by those who have devoted most of their big game shooting opportunities to this form of sport, so I cannot add much to it.

The tiger ruts at any time of the year, but more freely in the spring and at the beginning of the cold weather. The period of gestation is short, only fifteen weeks. Two or three cubs are born as a rule, but as many as six have been known. The

A sparsely marked tigress. Upper Burma.

A fine male tiger.

To face page 170.

tigress leaves the male before giving birth to her cubs in some secluded place, as the tiger is given to killing the cubs—even eating them on occasions.

Tigresses are dangerous when with cubs, and will attack freely in their defence. I have known of one follow up a party which had killed a half-grown cub in W. Siam, and give them three unpleasant nights in succession, coming right into camp, and putting every one up trees.

The cubs remain with the mother for two years, and will then often continue hunting together.

Dunbar Brander records having seen a party of six together, one old male, two tigresses and three big cubs. Also three full-grown males on another occasion.

Tigers are full grown at five to six years, but continue to "furnish" after that, the head in particular growing larger with age.

They probably live to about twenty-five years.

They demand water, shade and a certain amount of natural food, and are consequently confined to forest areas as a rule. They may, however, be found a considerable distance from their usual haunts, a notable instance of this being the tiger which killed Major Pritchard Taylor on the banks of a tank near Mhow in April 1926.

Tigers roar occasionally, but usually only when mating, and this is a different sound to the deep coughing "hough, hough" of a charging tiger. They also have a call very like the alarm note of a sambhar hind, which has been much discussed. Its purport is at present not known, but it is probably used for communication between two tigers hunting together.

I once had two tigers try and stampede my baggage ponies at night by roaring within about thirty yards of camp.

Their usual food is deer, such as sambhar and chital; in fact they are co-existent with sambhar nearly everywhere, even going as far as the extreme limit of the sambhar in the low rocky hills of Northern Jaipur. They also live extensively on village cattle, and often take to man-eating.

This last phase is one that calls for some comment. It used to be believed that only old worn-out beasts take to man-eating, but this is not so, though it may be the case, as is shown by the fact that three recently killed man-eaters of the Central Provinces were small, worn-out tigresses.

Man-eating may be hereditary, accidentally induced, or a local tendency.

Hereditary man-eating is probably caused by a tigress being hard put to it to feed her cubs, and finding man the easiest prey.

Man-eating may be accidentally induced by a tiger striking down a cattle-herd who gets in the way when the herd is being attacked.

A local tendency to man-eating may be caused in more than one way. In the northern Circars of Madras the destruction of deer by poachers has caused tiger to be short of natural food and man-eating to increase. In Eastern Assam, throughout Burma and W. Siam, it is as much man-killing as man-eating; for villages seldom suffer from a man-eater, while solitary men walking in the forest are often killed and carried off. Survey parties in Eastern Assam have suffered severely, while the telegraph line repair parties in Tenasserim and Mergui frequently have men killed by tigers. In fact I should say that tigers in these areas have a much more decided tendency to man-killing than anywhere else, but very rarely become regular man-eaters. It seems probable that tiger in these thinly populated and densely forested areas seldom see man and have acquired little respect for him, so kill him as a weak intruder into their domain.

They certainly show a boldness there, which the following incident will bear out. I was walking along a jungle path in W. Siam at midday in January 1924 carrying a ·280 Ross rifle, and with my terrier, Peter, trotting along eight or ten yards in front of me, when I saw something reddish moving in the forest about forty yards to my left front.

I turned over the safety catch of my rifle, hoping to get a barking deer for dinner, when a big tiger cantered out, making straight for my terrier. I fired at him as he cleared a fallen tree twenty-three yards away (I measured the distances later), hitting him low in the chest, and he charged me. Fortunately there was a tree four yards in front of me, and I side-stepped so that he had to swing to get at me, and hit him behind the shoulder as he did so. He came down on his chest, skidding past me in the dead leaves, rose again very sick, going straight on into the forest and disappearing within twenty yards. I waited until the elephants came up about forty-five minutes later, took a heavier rifle, and, after an unpleasant half-hour, found him dead in some thick grass about a hundred yards away.

This incident is notable in several ways. I have never heard of a tiger trying to take a small dog before, while his boldness and entire disregard of myself and the two Karens with me was amazing. It was also a lesson not to carry too light a rifle in tiger country, as, on examination, I found that that first bullet would almost certainly have killed him straight away if it had been a bit heavier, but it had broken up too soon. On skinning him I found a spherical bullet of hammered bronze embedded in the muscles of the left forearm. This had evidently been fired from a muzzle-loading Karen blunderbuss, and the result had very likely been the easy extinction of the owner, and a consequent rise in the tiger's morale, which may have been the reason for his boldness. He was a very heavy beast, measuring 9 feet 3 inches straight. The dressed skin now measures 10 feet 3 inches.

The usual method of bagging tiger is by beating, the preliminaries to it being the killing of a tied-up bait (buffalo or donkey) by the tiger, and marking him down into covert.

The bait should be tied up in the vicinity of thick covert and water, and the best season is the hot weather, when both are limited in quantity.

Tigers usually kill at night, and, after eating a portion of the carcase, beginning with the buttocks, it is dragged under shelter.

Sitting up is the only method possible very often in heavy and continuous forest, and there are no particular points that affect tiger more than any other animal.

Tracking is sometimes possible just after heavy rain, and is very fine sport. A tiger will usually stick to the more open ground under such circumstances, and will often lie down in some small open patch. If met with under such circumstances and at close range, it is often a moot point whether the tiger should be fired at: I think not, unless the hunter himself has not come into the open and has some possible cover, such as a tree-trunk, and also he must be very sure of his shooting. The tiger will usually stand for a few seconds facing the man, and then bound off into cover. He may, however, go away slowly (Dunbar Brander seems to infer that they usually do so in the Central Provinces, though that is not my experience in Burma), and give an easy forward raking shot.

They may be stalked at water-holes in the hot weather, or over a kill—natural or tied up—in the early morning or evening.

They are often hunted with dogs in the Nilgiris; in fact it is the usual method in outlying sholas (patches of jungle). The tiger is either driven out with the dogs keeping the beast at a slow pace, or bays inside the shola, when the gun can go in and shoot it. Tiger are likely to charge under such circumstances, as soon as they catch sight of a man.

I do not propose dealing with shooting tiger off elephant. It is a very fine tamasha and interesting to see, but does not come within the scope of this book.

It cannot be too strongly emphasised that, while an unwounded tiger is more often than not a harmless animal to man, there is no more dangerous beast than a wounded tiger. Wounded tigers must be followed up for the public good, and it must be done with care. A constant watch, men sent up trees to locate the animal, and the stoning of thick cover are essential precautions. A rest for a few minutes every half-hour is advisable to ease the strain and prevent relaxation of care. Steady shooting and a bold front are needed for the final act.

THE LEOPARD OR PANTHER

(*Felis pardus*)

Vernacular Names.—*Chitra*, *Chita*, Hindostani; *Sher*, N. Punjab; *Tendwa*, U.P.; *Gol Bagh*, Central India; *Palang*, Sind and Baluchistan; *Chinna-pillai*, S. India; *Hay*, Simla hills and Kumaon; *Kya-thit*, Burmese.

Description.—A detailed description of this well-known animal is unnecessary. The ground colour of the skin, number

LEOPARD WITH KILL.
(female Oorial).

AS HE FELL.

To face page 174.

and size of spots, and length of tail compared to body, all vary greatly with individual specimens, and in the same district, so that attempts have been made to establish more than one species, but have proved futile.

Having seen many from both countries, I have not been able to detect any consistent difference between Indian and African skins; in fact photographs I possess of leopards shot by me in Somaliland show just about as many and as large rosettes on the fore-quarters as in any Indian specimen, and weight, size and habits all correspond.

Black leopards are only examples of melanism, and occur (as do black wolves) in the same litter with cubs of ordinary colour. They are very scarce in N. and Central India, but not uncommon in the south.

The biggest leopard on record was killed in the Kashmir valley, and measured 8 feet 5¾ inches over the curves; probably about 8 feet, straight. Any leopard over 7 feet is a good specimen, and the big jungle "gol bagh" usually tapes well over this.

The leopards which hang round villages and prey largely on dogs and goats are usually small.

A 7-foot leopard will weigh about 115 lb.; one of 7 feet 2 inches shot by me in the Punjab Salt range weighed 121 lb.

Distribution.—Throughout the Indian Empire below 10,000 feet.

Habits and Characteristics.—The leopard is the largest vermin, and the most destructive and dangerous. They are prolific, not so much in the number of cubs born, which is two to four, but a larger proportion seem to come to maturity than with most carnivora.

They will kill and eat anything from man or buffalo to small bird or fish, and display wonderful cunning and perseverance in attacking their prey. They are wantonly destructive at times. I have known a leopard get into a small stone hut containing fifteen goats and kill fourteen of them without eating one; then, on the door being opened, dash out, upsetting the man who opened it.

They have been killed in big villages, on board ship (twice

to my knowledge), and in factory compounds; while I have known one take a dog from outside a cook-house door, at nine o'clock in the morning, with men of a British regiment all round it.

I have had one (in Somaliland) jump into my zareba, take a goat, and jump out, knocking over my cook; all within a few yards of me. In Burma one tried to scrape my terrier out from under my camp bed, while I was lying on it.

When they turn man-eater they are a greater scourge than a man-eating tiger. The Rudaprayag man-eater, killed in the Northern United Provinces in May 1926, had 125 human victims to its account, and almost held up the Upper Ganges pilgrim traffic. It was eventually killed by Captain Corbett, after twelve weeks' persistent effort and study of its habits, which gave the solitary and fleeting chance of a shot, of which he took advantage. A very fine performance. Numerous similar examples of man-eaters might be recounted.

Jungle leopards live principally on barking deer, monkeys, peafowl and young deer, but kill all the larger deer except adult sambhar and swamp deer stags; nothing smaller is safe from their attacks.

I once saw a stalk by a leopard from beginning to end. I was sitting about 11 A.M. near the centre of a big corrie in the Jhelum Salt range on the look out for an oorial ram, while five ewes were feeding about 200 yards away. I was examining a ridge some 500 yards distant with my glasses, when a big leopard came over the crest walking towards us. I particularly noticed that, except near the end of his tail, the spots did not show up separately at all, and he appeared uniformly grey. I think this explains the reports of snow leopards appearing in strange places in N. India, while the difficulty of seeing this particular animal made it quite evident that the value of his coloration for protective purposes is mainly at long ranges.

When he had come about 100 yards down the forward slope he spotted the oorial ewes feeding to my left front and a little below me, and immediately sat down, waving his tail with evident pleasure, and planning his stalk. About twenty seconds like this, and he started off gliding amongst the rocks and bushes, and looking about half his former size, eventually disappearing into a gully some thirty yards beyond the ewes. I then started forward to take a hand, but had only gone about 100 yards when I heard a feeble bleat from the direction of the ewes, and four of them bolted off. Walking a short distance down a ridge I soon saw the leopard standing over a dead ewe, in a small ravine, licking the neck of his kill. I sat down seventy yards away, and watching through my glasses for a couple of minutes, when the leopard picked up the ewe by the chest, and, without the slightest effort, jumped on to a big rock above him, then began pushing the kill in amongst the roots of a big thorn tree. I then shot him through the heart. I afterwards measured the rock on to which he had jumped with the ewe in his mouth, and it was well over 9 feet.

In this connection, I once knew a leopard jump out of a roofless den in a rajah's palace in Rajputana, where he was going to be made to fight a boar for my benefit. The wall was bare, smooth concrete, and, by measurement with a steel tape, 17½ feet high; yet he gripped the top of the coping with his forefeet, then jumped down an equal height into the stable-yard on the other side, and made off through the gate and up the neighbouring hill-side. This did not save him, however, for three or four of the rajah's shikaris pursued him up the hill-side and shot him with matchlocks.

Leopards are vermin which should be killed in every possible way, sitting up being probably the most successful. Sit up on the ground inside a shelter of branches or in a pit. The most favourable time of day is the half-hour on each side of sunset. A lamp may often be used to light the kill without deterring the leopard.

Beating is not so successful, as a leopard is wonderfully clever at breaking back, and also goes up a tree occasionally. I once had a casual beat from the left along a rocky hill-side, and a leopard, which had been lying up outside the beat and to my right, hearing it coming along, walked towards it with the evident intention of breaking through. He was seen by some men below me, and two or three of them came up and turned him out of the bushes in which he had squatted. He raced across my front, still going into the beat, and I killed him with my second shot.

N

I have tracked up and killed leopard in Somaliland three or four times, but there I had a couple of Somalis whom I trained, and who worked with me for years, while a good deal of light dust made conditions favourable. It was always done after a leopard had just fed heavily on a kill. I have never found conditions favourable for attempting it in India.

Leopards are wonderful climbers, and frequently place their kills high up in trees; even forty feet from the ground. They occasionally do not do this immediately, but after returning to a kill, and again not finishing it.

They begin to feed on the stomach of a kill as a rule, and nearly always clean out the carcase, and first eat the heart, liver and lungs, often half-burying the stomach.

A wounded leopard is a very dangerous animal, and it is amazing how slight the cover in which they will hide successfully. They charge with great determination, and inflict wounds with both teeth and claws which are very likely to go septic. Every care should be taken when shooting leopard or following them up. They will charge in defence of their cubs, and I have been attacked with great determination by a big male which was sleeping off a heavy gorge when I disturbed it.

They will usually grunt or emit a coughing roar when charging. The best-known noise of theirs is the "sawing" call, which is just like the thrust and recover of a big saw. Its purport is uncertain. Dunbar Brander thinks it is to encourage themselves on approaching a strange camp or house, but once in Burma I came on two leopards copulating at about 8 A.M., and was guided up to them by this call. I watched through the leaves for a little while, but they were moving about a lot, and eventually, in trying to get a better view, I stepped on some dry bamboos and frightened them off.

THE SNOW LEOPARD

(*Felis uncia*)

VERNACULAR NAMES.—*Safed chita*, Hindostani; *Bharal hé*, Spiti and the Sutlej valley.

DESCRIPTION.—This beautiful animal has a blue-grey ground colour on the upper parts and outside of the limbs and tail, this colour being heavily marked by irregular black rings filled in with a darker shade of the ground colour. The under parts are white. The fur is very soft and deep, the tail in particular being very thick. The length runs to a little over 7 feet, the best of many dressed skins I have seen being 8 feet 2 inches.

Distribution.—In the Indian Empire, the Himalayas, from Chitral to Nepal.

Habits and Characteristics.—Living at high altitudes and preying mainly on wild animals, the snow leopard is not very frequently shot, and then usually by chance. They live almost entirely on bharal and ibex in the summer, and, though they also kill a sheep or calf occasionally at that season, it is unusual. In the winter they come down into the valleys and attack the flocks, and it is then that most of the skins sold are obtained by trapping them in pitfalls. I have not heard of them coming below 7000 feet, and in summer they range to at least 18,000 feet in Ladakh.

I have only once seen a snow leopard. I was watching a herd of ibex through a powerful telescope, and a snow leopard suddenly raced across the hollow in which they were feeding and made an attempt on a buck, which started away just in time. The leopard's outstretched claws raked a great lump of hair from the ibex's coat as it wheeled away, and the whole herd bolted to the edge of the hollow, halting on a small ridge 100 yards away, and staring back at the leopard, which stood waving its great tail in the middle of the hollow. After a minute or so both parties departed in opposite directions. A very fine sight, but I regretted I was not able to take a hand, owing to a great steep-sided gulch between us.

Snow leopards seem to patrol ridge tops a good deal, as I have twice found a place where the melting snow at the crest had softened the soil, and there was a regular puddled path of leopard tracks going both ways. In one case, at about 15,000 feet near Lamayoro, there were a lot of wolf tracks amongst the leopard tracks.

Unfortunately, in both cases, the tracks were none of them very fresh; and, although I kept a good watch for two or three days, it was without result.

THE CLOUDED LEOPARD
(*Felis nebulosa*)

VERNACULAR NAMES.—*King*, Bhotia ; *Satchah*, Lepcha.

DESCRIPTION.—Like a small leopard about 6 feet in length, the clouded leopard is handsomely marked with large cloudy blotches instead of rosettes, on a yellowish-grey ground, the tail being ringed.

DISTRIBUTION.—In Nepal, Bhutan and Assam through Burma to Malaya.

HABITS AND CHARACTERISTICS.—This handsome cat is rare, and living as it does mainly in trees and in dense forests is seldom seen. It has very rarely been killed by any but natives.

It is often to be seen in zoos.

THE CARACAL
(*Felis caracal*)

VERNACULAR NAME.—*Siya Ghosh*, Hindostani.

DESCRIPTION.—Standing about 24 inches at the shoulder, the caracal is rather longer in the body and of lighter build than the Tibetan lynx. It is chestnut red in colour, has tasselled ears and a long tail.

DISTRIBUTION.—The Punjab, Sind and Rajputana, the southern portions of the United Provinces, and throughout the Central Provinces in suitable country.

I am sure that the caracal does not exist in Kashmir.

By misprint the Tibetan name " ee " for the lynx was converted into " ec " in Ward's *Sportsman's Guide to Kashmir*. This was taken by Burke and published in the *Indian Field Shikar Book* as " ech ", then repeated by Lydekker. The caracal is essentially an animal of hot, dry countries, and I have been unable to discover any evidence of its penetrating into the Himalayas, while its skin is never seen in the Srinagar skin shops.

HABITS AND CHARACTERISTICS.—The caracal is nowhere common, and is almost invariably found on stony, broken ground with a great deal of scrub jungle, or amongst sand and tamarisk.

Like the lynx it lives largely on hares and partridges, but has a more varied diet, probably due to greater opportunity. It seems to be commonest in Rajputana. I shot one once in the Punjab Salt range at about 3000 feet, and the local men did not recognise it, and had no name for it.

I have seen a good deal of this animal in Somaliland, and once had the pleasure of watching a couple of them stalking a covey of francolin. Unfortunately they caught sight of me and loped off, clearing a 7-foot thorn zareba side by side without any apparent effort.

THE TIBETAN LYNX

(*Felis lynx isabellina*)

VERNACULAR NAME.—*Ee*, Ladakh and Western Tibet.

DESCRIPTION.—A full-grown lynx stands about 24 inches, and weighs 60 lb. They are light sandy grey, infrequently marked with blurred spots. They have a handsome frill round the neck, and pointed ears. The tail is very short, and has earned them the name of "bob-cat". The tail and ears are tipped with black. The general build is very square and compact.

I have of recent years seen some very large skins up to 5½ feet in length in the Srinagar shops, and on inquiry have been unable to discover their origin. They are undoubtedly of a different race to the usual Ladakh skin (which does not run to more than 4 feet as a rule), and have a number of lighter spots, while the ground colour is redder. Whenever a Srinagar skin-merchant does not know where a skin comes from, he always answers "from Lhasa", and that is all the answer I could obtain.

DISTRIBUTION.—Most plentiful in the Upper Shyok and Rupshu district of Ladakh, this lynx is also found in Zanskar, Lahoul and Spiti. It does not seem to come below 10,000 feet, at which elevation I have seen it in the scrub jungle of the Shyok valley.

HABITS AND CHARACTERISTICS.—The lynx lives mainly on hares, partridges and pigeons, but also kills lambs. They are amazingly active, and, springing amongst a covey of partridge, will strike down three or four as they rise. They live in patches of willow-scrub, boortsia, or in clefts in the rocks. The cubs, two or three in number, are born in early summer. Once in July I came on a female lynx with three cubs at about 18,000 feet in the Hanle district. The woolly little cubs played happily within a few yards of me, while the mother stood anxiously watching about sixty yards away, occasionally making a mewing noise to call them to her. Eventually they joined her, and the family moved off together.

They tame easily, and make pleasant pets, but it is almost impossible to cure them of destroying fowls, or such like intruders, which may venture too near them.

The skins that come down for sale are almost exclusively from animals trapped in winter, pitfalls being the commonest form of trap.

THE CHITAH OR HUNTING LEOPARD

(*Cynaelurus jubatus*)

VERNACULAR NAME.—*Chitah* or *chitra*, Hindostani.

DESCRIPTION.—Superficially, the chitah resembles the ordinary leopard, but is at once distinguishable by being marked with solid spots instead of rosettes, by the long-legged light body, and the semi-retractile claws. They run to about 7 feet in length and 28 inches at the shoulder.

DISTRIBUTION.—It is exceedingly hard to get any recent information about this animal. The only one of which I have personal knowledge was shot in a beat near Nowgong in 1903. Since then they have been recorded from Hyderabad State, Berar and Kathiawar. They are evidently very scarce everywhere nowadays, and their distribution is probably limited to the south-west United Provinces, Kathiawar, Khandesh, Berar and Northern Hyderabad.

HABITS AND CHARACTERISTICS.—I have seen something of this animal in Somaliland, both wild and as pets. They are easily tamed, and safe and pleasant companions. Their habits in India are probably much what they are in Africa, that is, dwellers in dry country, with scrub jungle and broken ground as their favourite haunts.

They are, of course, famous in India as being kept by Indian chiefs to hunt blackbuck. Their speed is wonderful for a short distance, but they are easily ridden down well inside a mile.

They are generally inoffensive and timid animals.

THE STRIPED HYÆNA

(*Hyaena striata*)

VERNACULAR NAMES.—*Lakhar Baggar*, Hindostani; *Cherak*, Sindi; *Jhirak*, S. India; *Renhra*, Central India.

DESCRIPTION.—An unpleasant, furtive-looking animal, with high shoulders and drooping quarters, the striped hyæna stands about 26 inches, is a dirty grey striped with black, and has a crest running all along the back. In some districts where they go well up into high hills, they have quite handsome coats, but mostly they are very coarse, sparse, and often mangy.

DISTRIBUTION.—Almost throughout India, exclusive of Bengal and Assam and the further hills. Not in Burma or Malaya.

HABITS AND CHARACTERISTICS.—An unpleasant, slinking beast, mainly a carrion eater, but occasionally killing its own food, the hyæna lives in caves and thick jungle. I have seen a hyæna try and kill an oorial ewe in the Salt range, and also a chinkara in the Southern Punjab; but normally they are cowardly beasts, and, in spite of the immense power of their jaws, will not even fight when wounded.

They are rarely shot, as they are not usually considered worth a cartridge, but have occasionally been ridden and speared.

They are occasionally found in high crops, and mobbed to death by villagers, whose lambs and kids they destroy.

The power of their jaws is amazing, and the thigh-bone of a camel is splintered with the greatest ease.

THE WOLF

(*Canis lupus*)

THE INDIAN WOLF

(*Canis pallipes*)

VERNACULAR NAMES.—*Bheriar*, *Baggiar*, Hindostani; *Shanko*, Ladakh; *Gurk*, Baluchistan and Sind; *Bigara*, Central India.

DESCRIPTION.—I have purposely placed these two together, as I can find no satisfactory distinction laid down between the two species, and believe *Canis pallipes* to be a race of *Canis lupus*. A very big wolf I shot in Ladakh was 6 feet 3 inches long, and I saw one in the Punjab, while hunting oorial, which must have been nearly as big. The further south they live the smaller they seem to be, and a full-grown male shot by me in the United Provinces only measured 5 feet 0½ inches. The general colour is grey in Ladakh and light brown in Central India, but individuals vary a great deal, while there is nearly always more or less black on the back. Some skins are rufous in Central India, and this tinge does not seem to occur in the north of India. A yellowish shade may be found in skins from any part of India. One distinction that has been laid down is that the Indian wolf has no under-fur, but a skin has recently been obtained from Kangra which is in every other respect a typical *Canis pallipes*, but has a great deal of under-fur. The tail is comparatively short and bushy, about a quarter of the total length. Black wolves are common in Ladakh.

DISTRIBUTION.—Plentiful in Ladakh, Lahoul and Spiti, there are wolves to be found throughout the whole of Northern India, but they get scarcer further south. There was one killed near Coimbatore in 1902, but that is the furthest south I have known them occur. They are fairly common in the United Provinces. They avoid heavy forest and damp climates.

HABITS AND CHARACTERISTICS.—Wolves in Central India are justly hated and feared. They kill many small children, coming right into villages or snatching them up while herding goats. They seem particularly bad in the United Provinces and Hazaribagh. There were a couple near Nowgong in 1903 which killed over twenty children in one cold weather. I saw them once, and they appeared to be an old bitch and a young male, probably one of her cubs. They do not appear to be really dangerous to human life in other parts of India, but are very destructive to goats and sheep, and to blackbuck. I once saw an old wolf get a herd of sheep on the run in Ladakh and pull down five in thirty yards, seizing each one behind the right ear and jerking its head downwards and inwards so that it pitched on its nose and stunned itself, or broke its neck. The wolf then began to rip open the belly of the last one. It had already done this to a sheep which it had pulled down from the flock a little earlier.

They create great havoc amongst Tibetan gazelle and *Ovis ammon* if there is a heavy fall of snow, as the hoofed animal cannot then get about so fast.

They do not seem to hunt in large packs anywhere in India, and eight is the most that I heard of (in Hazaribagh) associating together regularly.

In Ladakh they hunt marmots in the summer, trying to cut them off from their holes while on grass-gathering expeditions.

THE WILD DOG

(*Cuon rutilans*)

VERNACULAR NAMES.—*Jangli kutta*, Hindostani ; *Ram hun*, Kashmir ; *Kolsa*, Marathi ; *Eram naikho*, Central India ; *Taw khwe*, Burma.

DESCRIPTION.—Standing about 22 inches, and with a total length of about 4½ feet (of which the tail is 15 inches), the wild dog is a bright foxy red above, changing to paler below. The colour may be also rufous-grey or rufous-brown. The tip of the tail is black as a rule, but sometimes white.

DISTRIBUTION.—Found in Northern India, exclusive of Sind ; it is scarce. It occurs very sparingly in the Kashmir valley, Kishenganga valley and Gilgit, and is recorded from

Ladakh and Spiti. Southwards it is found throughout the outer Himalayas, and plentifully in Central and Peninsular India; sparingly in Assam, Burma and Malaya.

HABITS AND CHARACTERISTICS.—This fierce little pest lives in packs, and destroys great quantities of game. It is usually found in forest country, and Lydekker's statement that "the destruction it inflicts on deer, wild sheep and chiru" is far-fetched, as it is so scarce in the outer Himalayas that I never even heard of it in the country where chiru and wild sheep are found. The statement by the same author that "In the Himalaya ibex form a large proportion of the prey of these animals" may be taken as having little or no foundation.

It is in Central and Southern India that they are plentiful enough to become a serious menace to the game. There they form large packs, up to thirty or more in number, are extremely prolific, having up to six pups in a litter, and hard to destroy.

They will face any animal in the jungle, even driving a tiger from his kill, and have been reported to kill a tiger. They destroy great numbers of sambhar hinds, which they run down with untiring energy, tearing at the flanks of the unfortunate beast.

I once saw four or five dogs running a sambhar hind across a hill-side in the Nilgiris. They were leaping at her belly, and occasionally getting a grip, then being flung off, but each time tearing a piece out of the unfortunate hind, which was rapidly weakening as the chase disappeared again in the forest.

Wild dogs are said to clear everything out of a forest in which they are hunting, and this certainly very often is the case, but I have seen half a dozen of them in the Nilgiris pass within twenty yards of grazing sambhar hinds, without either sambhar or dogs paying the slightest attention to each other. A very good and reliable observer also told me that he and another British officer were having lunch at a hill-top in the Nilgiris, and below were three sambhar hinds lying in the sun. Eight wild dogs came out of the forest and lay down within less than 100 yards of the hinds. About half-past three the sambhar rose and grazed towards the dogs, which shortly walked off past the hinds and within a few yards of them, no notice being taken by either.

Wild dogs are often very bold, and several can be shot out of a pack before they go off. Best (*Shikar Notes for Novices*) says that they can be called up by imitating the distressed bleat of a hind by blowing on the edge of a leaf held longitudinally between the thumbs. He has induced them to return more than once by this trick, after shooting one or more out of the pack.

Every possible means should be adopted to destroy these pests, but, as a rule, the rifle is the only effective weapon. Poison is difficult to use, both from the danger of other animals taking it, and from the fact that it is practically no use poisoning any but a freshly killed carcase, which is not often discovered.

THE HIMALAYAN BROWN BEAR

(*Ursus isabellinus*)

VERNACULAR NAMES.—*Lal bhalu*, Hindostani; *Shin harpat*, Kashmiri; *Drunmor*, Balti.

DESCRIPTION.—This bear runs to 7 feet in length, straight, for males, but the females are much smaller, and usually only tape about 5½ feet.

The coat is long and fine when new grown in the autumn before hibernation, and is then at its best. After hibernation, when the bears emerge in the spring, it is very matted and much coarser. It is shed through July and August, and they are not worth shooting until October. Females with cubs of the year have little or no hair on the under parts, and their skins are quite worthless.

The colour varies from dark brown, which is uncommon, to *café au lait*. I have never seen a coat of a colour which would justify the name of "red bear" by which they are so often called. Occasionally they are darker on the back, or have a white patch on the chest.

DISTRIBUTION.—From Waziristan and Afghanistan, throughout the Himalayas, to at least as far east as Nepal, and probably to the northern mountains of Burma.

Although almost exterminated in the more accessible parts of its habitat, they still flourish in many of the remoter mountains. They are even still to be found in at least three valleys on the south side of the Kaj-i-Nag, on both sides of the Pir Panjal, and in Kulu.

Lydekker states that they are non-existent in the Dras valley, which is a very good locality for them; and in Suru, where they are on the increase. They also seem to be increasing in Baltistan of late years, and they are again beginning to turn up on the Deosai plateau.

The bears from Kishtwar and Chamba seem to run larger than those from the Shamshibri and Baltistan.

HABITS AND CHARACTERISTICS.—Appearing to graze on open grassy slopes in late April or early May, the brown bear is very easy to shoot, as he crawls about on some sunlit patch of grass after his winter fast. They then follow the melting snow right up to the permanent line, living by grazing until the grass gets too coarse for their taste. In August and September they dig for roots, ploughing up big patches of rich vegetation near the upper tree-line. At the end of September many of them descend and loot the higher fields of Indian corn and patches of autumn berries; while, about this time, some of the old males adopt unpleasant carnivorous habits, and are destructive to cattle and sheep. They have a revolting trick (black bear also do this) of mauling a pony or cow until it can no longer move, and then beginning to feed on it while it is still alive. I have seen two instances of this, and was able to shoot one brute myself, while the other was tracked into a cave and smothered by a big fire lit by some villagers, and I saw his singed carcase extracted. I had no sympathy whatever after having seen his wretched victim.

They will also, in the spring, dig out the bodies of ibex killed in the winter avalanches and devour them.

The females and young ones seem to stay up high, as a rule, in autumn, and devote themselves mainly to digging out and eating the stores of roots amassed by voles, the unfortunate owners being also considered as *bonnes bouches*.

Once, in late October, and in a remote part of eastern Kashmir, I found a hill-side scarred with digging, and discovered the perpetrators to be an old female brown bear, with a family of a couple of cubs of the previous year, and one cub of the year.

BROWN BEAR.

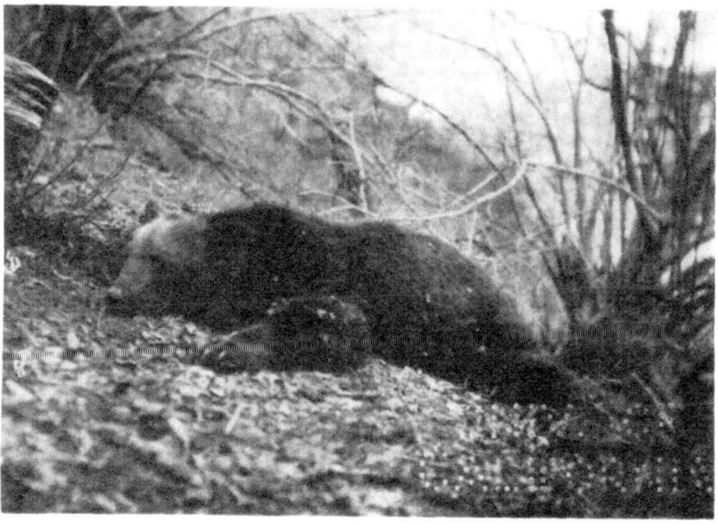

BLACK BEAR.

To face page 188.

It was most interesting watching the party dig out voles. Stones weighing 30 lb. or more were sent flying with a jerk of the forearm, and the dig always ended in the same way—with one paw working away hard and the other poised to catch the vole as it made a last bid for safety. Then down would come the upraised paw on the little beast, and it would be bolted with obvious relish, the store of roots being then pulled out and devoured. The yearling cub used to come begging to mamma, after doing a little digging on his own, and once, when the old lady had trapped a vole, he tried to push his nose in under her paw and eat it, the result being that she gave him such a box on the ear as would almost have taken the head off a man, and sent him rolling down the hill with a yelp. I had managed to get into a clump of rhododendrons a few yards away, and was vastly entertained by the whole performance.

Brown bears often climb trees for berries, especially a tall, rowan-like tree which grows profusely in eastern Kashmir. I once saw two two-year-old bears grubbing about close to a fallen log, and stalked up behind it to try and take their photographs. Just as I got there they both climbed up a rowan tree about 25 feet high, and began feeding on the berries. I dashed underneath and began to take photos, one of them dropping out of the tree almost immediately and bolting ; the other would not face it, but remained up there shaking a branch and singing a sort of psalm at me. I called up the Kashmiri shikari and told him we would try to catch the youngster (who was about the size of a collie dog) in the tiffin cooli's blanket, and made him take one end while I took the other. I then kicked the tree, and it was too much for the youngster's nerves, so down he dropped, plumb into the blanket. The shikari promptly threw away his end and fled, so I chucked mine over the cub and tried to collar him. I felt as if I had tried to wrestle with a well-armed cyclone, and after I had lost a good deal of skin and nearly all my shirt, the little beast went off down the hill through the trees howling like a lost soul. I had to get a new blanket for the tiffin cooli.

Pairing takes place in October as a rule, and the cubs are born, in February probably, during hibernation.

They are usually two in number, but one is frequent.

They stay with the mother over one full winter, and until the succeeding autumn, probably hibernating apart from her but close by. If there are two cubs they often stay together for another year or two after leaving the mother.

All brown bear in the Himalayas go into hibernation as soon as the first heavy snow falls at about 8000 feet, a hollow below the roots of some big tree being a favourite spot.

Brown bear are very easy to shoot, as they are practically entirely dependent on their sense of smell for defence against man. They have wonderful noses, but their eyesight is so poor that I have twice walked up to one, and once to two bears, on an open grassy slope, to within seventy yards of them. Whenever they raised their heads to look at me, I simply kept still; and, after sitting up in a foolish way to look at me, they decided that I was some kind of tree, and went on feeding.

In the end of October 1919, heavy snowfalls drove the bears down off the Shamshibri range, and, at about 8000 feet, I shot a brown and a black bear right and left. Next day I went up again, and shot the female brown bear, which was eating her husband's carcase, from which the skin had been stripped. She had a very curious coat, as there was no long hair, except in the region of head and neck, the body being entirely covered with extra thick "pushm", as the fine under-coat is called.

Brown bears are hardly dangerous, unless the hunter is very careless, so be merciful and do not shoot too many.

THE SLOTH BEAR

(*Melursus ursinus*)

VERNACULAR NAMES.—*Bhalu*, Hindostani; *Rinch*, S.E. Rajputana and Western U.P.; *Aswal*, Central India; *Kard-adi*, Tamil.

DESCRIPTION.—A long and very coarse black coat; elongated, almost naked snout, and very powerful, long claws, are the principal features of the sloth bear. The snout and spectacles are dirty grey, and there is a white chevron patch on the chest as in the Himalayan black bear.

The hair on the shoulders is longer and shaggier than elsewhere, so adding to the clumsy, untidy appearance of the animal. A big male bear will measure 6 feet, a female about 5 feet.

DISTRIBUTION.—All Peninsular India (and Ceylon), then northwards into Rajputana and the foot of the Himalayas, up to Northern Bengal. Not found in Assam or Burma.

HABITS AND CHARACTERISTICS.—A clumsy, guzzling, dangerous clown, the sloth bear is rightly feared for its bad temper by Indian villagers. Hard of hearing, and short-sighted, some unfortunate woodcutter is liable to stumble on it in thick bush, when asleep or feeding, and have his face torn in pieces and be mauled in ghastly fashion.

Broken country, with caves and patches of thick cover, is what they like, and their food consists of many kinds of jungle fruit, grubs, honey, white ants and mohwa flowers. They dig with extraordinary rapidity. I have seen one just commencing on an ant-hill, and then be more than half inside it when I arrived less than ten minutes later. Fruit is, however, their principal diet, and they will go about in parties from clump to clump, snuffling and grunting, throughout the night. They may be found feeding at any hour, but are largely nocturnal. They go up as high as 6000 feet in the Nilgiris, and there used to be a clump of wild plum trees outside a little bungalow on the crest of the Hulikal Drug at about that elevation, which, when in fruit, was visited regularly by them.

They are occasionally found in cultivation quite a long way from cover, when attracted by ber trees in fruit.

They must have a very keen sense of smell when hunting for food, as Dunbar Brander records one digging out a single grub, from what would appear to have been a depth of at least 18 inches.

Like the Himalaya black bear, they emit a weird howling chant when hit, and also attack a companion with the idea that he is responsible for the damage.

They have also a curious trick of sucking a fore-paw and emitting a loud humming noise, which may be heard at some distance. Dunbar Brander suggests that this is done to ease bruises acquired in digging or turning over stones, but I have often seen both sloth and Himalaya black bears doing this in zoos, where this could hardly be the reason. I have never, however, heard or seen the Himalaya black bear doing this in the wild state.

Sloth bears are still plentiful throughout the forests of the Central Provinces and parts of the United Provinces, Behar, Orissa and the Northern Circars, but less so in Southern India.

They are usually shot in beats or driven out of caves by fireworks, but the pleasantest way to tackle them is stalking by moonlight. They can be found feeding on wild plums or mohwa flowers, or intercepted on their way from one clump to another.

They are very noisy and rough when at play or courting, and frequently bear marks of each other's caresses.

The female often carries a cub, or two of them, on her back, and looks like an exceptionally big and short specimen when galloping along.

Bears are clumsy and slow movers and should not be very dangerous to any steady shot, but it is not advisable to fire when directly below them on a slope.

Always hold low. The shaggy hair on the back makes them appear much bigger than they are.

THE MALAY BEAR

(*Ursus malayanus*)

Vernacular Names.—*Wet-wun*, Burma ; *Bruan*, Malay.

Description.—This little bear is short-coated and long-bodied, with no ruff. The chevron on the chest is usually yellow or even orange, but may be white. They run to 4½ feet in length, but are lightly built, and probably never weigh more than 80 lb.

Distribution.—It is difficult to discover the Northern and Western limits of this bear. Lydekker states that it occurs in Arakan and the Garo hills, but I have been unable to get reliable information of its occurrence there. In the Irrawadi catchment area it seems to exist well up the Chindwin and to the top of the Ruby Mines district, but only turns up very occasionally in those districts. In the lower Salween valley it is fairly common, but Tenasserim and Mergui are the most likely places to find it. I have seen it in the Tenasserim hills at nearly 4000 feet.

HABITS AND CHARACTERISTICS.—Although easily distinguished from the Himalayan bear, which is co-existent with it almost throughout its habitat in the Indian Empire, the Malay bear is frequently confused with it. The latter, in spite of its small size, is reported to be very ferocious. They climb trees with great rapidity in quest for food. Their food seems to be mainly fruit and insects, but local Karens credit them with being very destructive to birds' nests.

Evergreen jungle seems to be a necessity of its existence.

BLACK HIMALAYAN BEAR

(*Ursus torquatus*)

VERNACULAR NAMES.—*Kala bhalu*, Hindostani ; *Rinch*, Punjab and Poonch and Central India ; *Harpat*, Kashmir ; *Wet-won*, Burmese.

DESCRIPTION.—Covered with long, coarse hair, this bear is black all over, except for a white crescent mark on the chest. Males run up to about 6 feet in length (straight), and a weight of 400 lb. Females up to 5 feet 4 inches in length, and 200 lb. weight.

DISTRIBUTION.—From North-Western Sind right round the N.W. Frontier, through Baluchistan, Waziristan and the hills north-west of Peshawar, then through the Upper Swat and middle Indus valleys to Kashmir, where it is particularly plentiful. It ranges all along the outer Himalayas, through Nepal, Bhutan, Assam and Burma to Siam, where I obtained the only specimen known from that country.

The biggest specimens come from W. Kashmir, and old males from Baluchistan and Tenasserim (the extremes of its habitat) only tape about 4½ feet in length.

HABITS AND CHARACTERISTICS.—Black bear stick largely to forest country, and do not cross into the barren ranges on the further slopes of the Himalayas. They feed on grass and crops, but eat fruit, berries and roots, while old males are often most destructive to sheep. Insects and honey are also eaten.

They are particularly fond of maize, and the damage they do in the fields at night is great in some districts. Walnuts and mulberries are also favourite food. They climb to great heights after berries, and I have seen their traces up to quite 75 feet from the ground.

Unlike the brown bear, they dig very little in the Himalayas, but a great deal in Burma.

They only partially hibernate, and may appear during any spell of mild weather in Kashmir, and come down as low as 3000 feet in the Chenab valley. I have never seen them over 10,500 feet, and only twice at such a height. In Burma and Siam they come down as low as 1200 feet above sea-level.

Black bear can be exceedingly dangerous, sometimes attacking unprovoked, if suddenly met with at close quarters. They are, however, clumsy and slow movers, except downhill. Fearful wounds may sometimes be seen made by bears encountered unexpectedly in maize fields or jungle, and they maul the head and shoulders with great ferocity. I have known several black bears which took regular toll of sheep, and lived largely on a flesh diet. One I shot in May 1926 was said to have destroyed over 300 sheep and a score of cows; while he killed one man and crippled another for life. This was a very big bear, taping 5 feet 10 inches straight, and pegging out at 7 feet 8 inches. He certainly weighed over 400 lb. Although shot early in the year, when bear are usually thin after the short commons of winter, this beast was in splendid condition. I found two old bullets and three lead slugs in him on taking off the skin.

Once, early in September, I was camped at about 10,000 feet in Eastern Kashmir, and we had five days' steady rain and mist. There was a big sheepfold about 200 yards from my tent, and two black bears attacked this on three successive nights. Their method was to break into the fold and stampede the sheep, then hunt and kill them in the darkness. Once a bear passed through the ropes of my tent in pursuit of sheep, and in the three nights they killed forty-two.

The rut is in October, and the courting is rough in the extreme. I once shot a female bear which had been flirting round my camp the previous night, and the noise the two made was explained when I found that she had her lip bitten through in three places and other deep tooth-marks on her face, while her back had also been severely clawed and bitten. I got the male, and he had several similar marks of affection.

The cubs are born in late winter or early spring, and there are usually two, though I have twice seen three.

The cubs stay with their mother until the succeeding winter, and, if there is not another family, very often for a further year.

It is very amusing watching an old female urging back her family to cover after feeding out too late in the morning. She utters curious little admonitory grunts and scoldings to the cubs, which persist in wandering to investigate strange objects, until finally she loses her temper and gives one a box on the ear which rolls him over with a howl.

Black bears are most usually shot in beats, but the most interesting method is to catch them on the young grass in spring. Sitting up at night for them is now forbidden in Kashmir, as it caused too many fatalities to cattle, which were shot in mistake for bears.

They are often found in caves, sometimes three or four together, and their winter nests are usually in hollows under roots or rocks, and they generally lie up for the day in summer in similar places or in patches of thick scrub.

They are very fast climbers. I once came on a bear suddenly in pine forest, and he went 40 feet up a big " Kail " pine in a few seconds. He then got out on to a big transverse branch, and, gripping the stem with all four feet and with his body at right angles to it, he jerked the branch up and down, singing a sort of chanting combination service at me. I sat down about thirty yards away, and he repeated this performance every few minutes until, after about half an hour, he could stand it no longer, and climbed rapidly down, dropping the last 15 feet, then bundling off into the forest.

Do not take liberties with bears: I very nearly came to grief through doing so. They are clumsy, rather ridiculous and easily stalked; but they are not too easy to kill clean owing to their indefinite shape, making decisive aim hard to take, and they will charge home and inflict ghastly injuries.

Like sloth bear, they nearly always give tongue when hit, and will attack a companion who happens to be close to them, under the impression that the injury comes from him.

Avoid firing when a bear is straight above you. They always bolt downhill, travelling very fast, and go for any living thing they meet.

INDEX

THE END